Language Teaching:
A Scheme for Teacher Education

Editors: C N Candlin and H G Widdowson

Writing

Christopher Tribble

Oxford University Press
1996

Oxford University Press
Great Clarendon Street, Oxford OX2 6DP

Oxford New York
Athens Auckland Bangkok Bogota Bombay
Buenos Aires Calcutta Cape Town Dar es Salaam
Delhi Florence Hong Kong Istanbul Karachi
Kuala Lumpur Madras Madrid Melbourne
Mexico City Nairobi Paris Singapore
Taipei Tokyo Toronto

and associated companies in
Berlin Ibadan

OXFORD and OXFORD ENGLISH
are trade marks of Oxford University Press

ISBN 0 19 437141 7

© Oxford University Press 1996

Typeset by Wyvern Typesetting Ltd, Bristol

Printed in Hong Kong

To my parents
Phyllis and Albert Tribble

Contents

The author and series editors

Christopher Tribble has an MA in Applied Linguistics from the University of London Institute of Education and is now completing Ph.D research into writing in corporate organizations. Between 1992 and 1995 he was the English Language Teaching Consultant and Projects Manager for the new British Council Directorate in the Baltic States. He is now a freelance lecturer and consultant.

Christopher N Candlin is Professor of Linguistics in the School of English, Linguistics, and Media, and Executive Director of the National Centre for English Language Teaching and Research at Macquarie University, Sydney, having previously been Professor of Applied Linguistics and Director of the Centre for Language in Social Life at the University of Lancaster. He also co-founded and directed the Institute for English Language Education at Lancaster, where he worked on issues in in-service education for teachers.

Henry Widdowson is Professor of English for Speakers of Other Languages at the University of London Institute of Education, having previously been Lecturer in Applied Linguistics at the University of Edinburgh. Before that, he worked on materials development and teacher education as a British Council English Language Officer in Sri Lanka and Bangladesh.

Through work with The British Council, The Council of Europe, and other agencies, both Editors have had extensive and varied experience of language teaching, teacher education, and curriculum development overseas, and both contribute to seminars, conferences, and professional journals.

Introduction

Writing

This book—like the others in the series—is divided into three sections. Section One deals with important issues in the development of theories for the teaching of writing. Emphasis has been given here to two apparently contrasting approaches, one associated with the *processes* of writing, and the other, often called a genre approach, with the demands made by the *contexts* in which writing takes place. During recent years there has been a degree of debate, at times heated, between proponents of one approach or the other. This book argues for a pedagogy that draws on the considerable strengths of both views of writing instruction.

The second section of the book looks at currently available teaching materials in the light of the discussion in Section One, and proposes a set of criteria which teachers can use when they are evaluating the potential usefulness of published materials for their own teaching situations. The emphasis here is on building a practical framework for evaluation rather than on providing a survey review. Thus two key areas in writing instruction—Business Communication and Foreign Language Teaching for Academic or Study Purposes—are taken as case studies. Another important aspect of teaching writing, responding to student writing, is also considered. This is something that is not usually covered in detail in instructional materials, but is clearly of great significance for teachers.

Section Three of *Writing* offers readers an opportunity to test in their own classrooms some of the ideas that have been discussed. Much of the value of this series seems to me to lie in the way in which current thinking on matters of importance in language teaching is presented to language teachers in a manner that encourages further investigation in the specific conditions of *their* classrooms. Section Three, therefore, contains a number of practical research activities which should make it possible for student teachers or experienced professionals to extend their understanding of this important language skill.

This book begins with the question 'Why teach writing?', and goes on to discuss why a language skill that is mastered by so few should form part of a foreign language syllabus. I hope that the book will lead readers to feel that the whole project of writing instruction *is* worthwhile and rewarding. I certainly think it is, although writing a book about writing has been an experience in which I have often had to take my own medicine, especially when it has come to the process of drafting and revision.

I would like to express my gratitude, therefore, to Susan Maingay, who has read the complete manuscript at various points in its development in an attempt to ensure that I make sense most of the time, and to my former colleagues Colin Campbell, Karen Giblin, and Brian Maguire—British Council ELT Consultants in Estonia, Latvia, and Lithuania respectively—who have had to listen to many of the arguments that have been developed in the book during long drives through the Baltic countries. I would also like to thank the series editors, Professors Chris Candlin and Henry Widdowson for their professional and personal support. At a distance, Chris Candlin has provided trenchant and constructive comments which have tightened my arguments in many essential ways. Henry Widdowson was my teacher in the Institute of Education and has continued to be a guiding influence. Part of the pleasure of writing this book has been the opportunity of continuing the discussions which we began in 1984. He is an exceptional teacher, a stimulating editor, and certainly the most perceptive reader a writer could ever wish for.

As is customary in the genre of introductions, my last task is to declare that any infelicities or failings in this book are mine and mine alone. However, if the book works, it is thanks to the readers who had already responded to it many times before it went to press.

Language Teaching:
A Scheme for Teacher Education

The purpose of this scheme of books is to engage language teachers in a process of continual professional development. We have designed it so as to guide teachers towards the critical appraisal of ideas and the informed application of these ideas in their own classrooms. The scheme provides the means for teachers to take the initiative themselves in pedagogic planning. The emphasis is on critical enquiry as a basis for effective action.

We believe that advances in language teaching stem from the independent efforts of teachers in their own classrooms. This independence is not brought about by imposing fixed ideas and promoting fashionable formulas. It can only occur where teachers, individually or collectively, explore principles and experiment with techniques. Our purpose is to offer guidance on how this might be achieved.

The scheme consists of three sub-series of books covering areas of enquiry and practice of immediate relevance to language teaching and learning. Sub-series 1 focuses on areas of *language knowledge*, with books linked to the conventional levels of linguistic description: pronunciation, vocabulary, grammar, and discourse. Sub-series 2 (of which this present volume forms a part) focuses on different *modes of behaviour* which realize this knowledge. It is concerned with the pedagogic skills of speaking, listening, reading, and writing. Sub-series 3 focuses on a variety of *modes of action* which are needed if this knowledge and behaviour is to be acquired in the operation of language teaching. The books in this sub-series have to do with such topics as syllabus design, the content of language course, and aspects of methodology and evaluation.

This sub-division of the field is not meant to suggest that different topics can be dealt with in isolation. On the contrary, the concept of a scheme implies making coherent links between all these different areas of enquiry and activity. We wish to emphasize how their integration formalizes the complex factors present in any teaching process. Each book, then, highlights a particular topic, but also deals contingently with other issues, themselves treated as focal in other books in the series. Clearly, an enquiry into a mode of behaviour like speaking, for example, must also refer to aspects of language knowledge which it realizes. It must also connect to modes of action which can be directed at developing this behaviour in learners. As elements of the whole scheme, therefore, books cross-refer both within and across the different sub-series.

This principle of cross-reference which links the elements of the scheme is also applied to the internal design of the different inter-related books within it. Thus, each book contains three sections, which, by a combination of text and task, engage the reader in a principled enquiry into ideas and practices. The first section of each book makes explicit those theoretical ideas which bear on the topic in question. It provides a conceptual framework for those sections which follow. Here the text has a mainly *explanatory* function, and the tasks serve to clarify and consolidate the points raised. The second section shifts the focus of attention to how the ideas from Section One relate to activities in the classroom. Here the text is concerned with *demonstration*, and the tasks are designed to get readers to evaluate suggestions for teaching in reference both to the ideas from Section One and also to their own teaching experience. In the third section this experience is projected into future work. Here the set of tasks, modelled on those in Section Two, are designed to be carried out by the reader as a combination of teaching techniques and action research in the actual classroom. It is this section that renews the reader's contact with reality: the ideas expounded in Section One and linked to pedagogic practice in Section Two are now to be systematically *tested out* in the process of classroom teaching.

If language teaching is to be a genuinely professional enterprise, it requires continual experimentation and evaluation on the part of practitioners whereby in seeking to be more effective in their pedagogy they provide at the same time—and as a corollary—for their own continuing education. It is our aim in this scheme to promote this dual purpose.

Christopher N Candlin
Henry Widdowson

Explanation

1　Why teach writing?

1.1　Introduction

An ability to *speak* well—fluently, persuasively, appropriately—is something that most of us would hope to achieve in our first language. It is also an objective for many learners of a foreign language, especially those who wish to do business internationally, or to study or travel in English speaking countries. An ability to *write* appropriately and effectively is, however, something which evades many of us, in our mother tongues or in any other languages we may wish to learn, and this in spite of the many years which are frequently devoted to the development of the skill. The reasons for this difficulty will be considered in detail in later sections of this book, where we will touch on issues such as the artificial, learned nature of the skill of writing itself, and the way in which written language has developed in urban, technologically oriented societies in order to deal with complex intellectual and social tasks. For the moment we can accept that writing is a language skill which is difficult to acquire. It is, furthermore, one in which relatively few people are required to be expert. So why teach it?

▶　TASK 1

Given below are the profiles of three students, all of whom have to follow language programmes of one sort or another. On the basis of the information given here, decide what reasons a teacher of English might have for including writing in each of these student's courses.

1　*Larissa Skopinskaya.* Larissa is nineteen and works in the Personnel Department of a St Petersburg bank. She is studying for an internationally recognized English language examination in order to get herself a new job with a multinational organization.

2　*Nussrat Begum.* Nussrat is a twelve-year-old girl who lives in Toronto, Canada. She has recently arrived in Canada from India (her first language is Punjabi), and will take national school examinations in four years' time.

3　*Charles Nolotshungo.* Charles, who is thirty-two, lives in South Africa and works in the Public Health Department of Cape

Town City Council. His education has been interrupted because of social disruption so he is studying English as part of an evening course in accountancy. He also wants to set up his own firm.

For Larissa, writing has a low priority at the moment. She comes from a highly literate culture and, in her first language, has a well-established capacity to write the sorts of texts that are required by her present job. She feels that spoken English is her primary need. At present, she wants to be able to answer the phone, to greet visitors, and to understand when she hears things in English. This will be particularly important if she is to receive training in English in her new job. What she may not realize is that a great deal of the work she will be doing will also depend on written documents—memos, reports, letters, faxes—and that she is not yet capable of writing this sort of document effectively. Her confident and relatively fluent spoken English will not transfer directly to the written mode. The inclusion of writing in her course of study might also be justified for language-learning reasons, on the grounds that it will help her to focus on accuracy and remember things that arise in class. She will also need to write in her examination. Confidence in certain types of writing, especially the preparation of short factual reports, will be of real use to Larissa as her career develops. As a woman in a business community where the managerial class is predominantly male, it will be helpful if Larissa is able to write policy-forming documents as well as administrative texts. Such a skill might well give her a significant advantage as she progresses in her career.

Nussrat is at the beginning of her education in Canada. Although her parents can read and write in their first language, they are not confident in English and cannot help Nussrat in her school studies. In spite of their own problems with the language, they feel strongly that a command of English and the development of literacy skills are very important for their daughter because they see these skills as a key to entering a professional class which is barred to them. Nussrat's parents also feel that she has to catch up with her English-speaking classmates and get ready for national examinations four years ahead. In this case, the teaching of writing will not be an immediate priority: the first objective is to help Nussrat settle into school and begin to feel comfortable with classmates and the daily routine of learning. The development of reading and writing skills will, however, need to be included early on in the programme to help Nussrat consolidate her language learning.

For Charles, developing an ability to write fluently and confidently in English is a high priority; he needs now to develop the literacy skills denied him before so that he can take advantage of the changed circumstances in the new South African Republic. Charles has bookkeeping experience and now wants to complete his professional training so that he can get work in one of the newly-established international companies, and eventually set up his own firm. He knows that he has got to be able to write effectively if he is going to achieve his aims. A teacher designing a course for Charles will give immediate priority to the practical writing skills which will give him a chance of access to the professional opportunities he seeks.

1.2 What to teach?

The case studies in Task 1 give an indication of some of the issues that we face if we ask ourselves the question 'Why teach writing?' They also show why this question is not likely to produce a simple answer. There are many types of writing and many reasons for learning to write. Of course, for some students, and this can apply to both Foreign Language (FL) and Second Language (SL) learners, there may not be a strong reason for teaching them to write in a foreign language as they are unlikely to find themselves involved in the social roles that require this skill. But for others, writing will be an essential component in the learning programme. As teachers, we have to find ways of helping our students to decide on their priorities and then agree on what the focus of a learning programme will be. In the context of teaching writing, this involves not only the questions 'Why?' and 'How?' It also involves the question 'What?'

 ### TASK 2

Which of the following kinds of text do you feel it would be important for the majority of people to be able to write in their first language? Which kinds of text are likely to be relevant for second language learners?

advertisement	*novel*
essay	*newspaper article*
filling in a form	*Ph.D thesis*
journal article	*poem*
laboratory report	*pop-song lyric*
letter to a bank manager	*postcard*
letter to a business contact	*report*
letter to a newspaper	*shopping list*
letter to their mother or father	*story*
note about a telephone message	*technical manual*

If you feel that *all* of these are important targets for first language learners, you are perhaps aiming a little high. Most of us could not—and would not need to—write effectively across such a broad range of types of writing. Most people can get through their lives very effectively with an ability to write little more than a shopping list, the odd message, and a letter or postcard, and to fill in official documents such as income tax forms. A few of us might have to write reports; very few of us ever need to write essays, manuals, novels, or newspaper articles.

For language learners, the list of texts is likely to be much shorter. Letters to family or friends are not usually written in a foreign language. Neither are shopping lists, telephone messages, or poems. The things that students may need to write in a foreign language are more probably going to be essays, reports, or even Ph.D theses. By the same token, they are more likely to have to write to a business partner in a foreign language than they are to their bank manager. The role of written English in the lives of most second and foreign language learners is very different from the one it occupies in the lives of people who use English as their mother tongue. This is something that we will have to bear in mind in any consideration of the teaching of writing.

As a final comment on this list, it is also worth thinking about what students *want* to write as opposed to what they *have* to write. If we ask our students this question, we may find that poems, advertisements, and pop-song lyrics come at the top. What will motivate students may be very different from the things that they are obliged to do!

 ## TASK 3

All of the activities below can be described as 'writing'. Which of them might be included in a writing course for students who are learning a foreign language?

1 A child is copying a row of repeated letter 'c' and 's' into her exercise book, making sure that she is linking them together exactly as shown in the model.

2 A medical doctor is transferring a set of interview notes from a notebook onto a word-processor and adding comments as she goes.

3 A man is sitting under a tree. He is writing on a piece of paper the words 'Chapter 1 . . .'

4 A student is sitting at a desk in an examination room. She writes: 'This question can be answered in several ways . . .'

5 A man is sitting in a hotel room. He is writing postcards to friends in another country.

The examples above represent very different sorts of activity, requiring very different skills. Some—1 and 4 for example—can be seen as necessary preparation for the complex adult tasks given in 2 and 3. However, 4 might be the only type of writing that the student ever needs to do in a foreign language and could represent the end point in this particular student's career as a writer in that language. She may never need or want to be able to write to friends in the way that the man in example 5 is doing. Similarly, a student whose first language uses the Roman alphabet will not need to go through the preparatory phase being undertaken by the girl in example 1 when he or she begins to write in a language like English. Another problem that we have to deal with then, is which aspects of the activity called 'writing' we need to address in different language learning classrooms.

1.3 Different students: different needs

▶ TASK 4

A group of European teachers of EFL were asked to give reasons for including writing in their teaching programmes. Their responses are set out below. Would you give the same reasons? Why do you think that the teachers felt obliged to divide their responses into two main groups, one dealing with students in the school system, the other dealing with adult learners?

School students	*Adult learners*
to give opportunities for language practice (review grammar and vocabulary)	to give opportunities for language practice (review grammar and vocabulary)
to allow teachers to focus on accuracy	to allow students and teachers to focus on accuracy, and also to allow students to extend their knowledge of the language independently
it will be of future professional benefit (Business English)	because students have a professional need to write (business or academic purposes)
because students have to write in EFL examinations	because students have to write in EFL examinations
to give opportunities for creative/imaginative language use	
because it has a general educational value—it can help students become 'better writers in their first language	

The set of comments in the left-hand column gives an insight into some of the roles that writing takes on in most school systems. Traditionally, one of these is to provide a way of checking on the students' understanding of what has been taught; most exams are written, or have a significant written component. This accounts for the responses 'to give opportunities for language practice (review grammar and vocabulary)' and 'to allow . . . teachers to focus on accuracy'. However, language practice can also be provided by giving students opportunities for creative language use. This, too, can develop writing as an enabling skill, although it may lead to problems when writing is used in assessment, where the focus is often on accuracy.

The other comments are of interest as they give us an idea of the way English works both in society and in the school system, and they emphasize learning *purpose*. The justification 'it will be of future professional benefit (Business English)' hints at the status of English as a medium for international communication. As teachers, we know that we have to prepare students for life beyond school. Whether we are always clear about what is meant by 'business' writing is another question. The comment about examinations highlights the sort of circularity that can happen when assessment gets mixed up with syllabuses: 'We teach it because it's examined'. It also begs the question of what sort of writing ought to be taught or tested.

Issues such as educational disability, age, or the problems faced by students who are transferring from one script system to another may limit the writing component in language teaching programmes for secondary school students, but it is difficult to imagine the complete exclusion of writing at this level.

Turning to the comments given to justify the teaching of writing skills to adult students, it appears that these are more closely determined by the learning styles and purposes of adults than is the case with learners in the school system. When the teachers in the study talked about 'accuracy' and 'practice' they referred to the way in which writing lets students focus on accuracy and encourages independent language development. When they talked about the professional need to learn how to write, they focused on current rather than future needs. Although oral fluency remains the main objective for most adult language learners, becoming a proficient writer has also become a major objective for many students, especially for those who want to become members of the international business, administrative, or academic communities.

1.4 Conclusion

It should now be clear that language teachers need to be aware of a broad range of relevant issues if they are to have a reasoned basis for teaching writing. These include the nature of writing, its role in society, and how it is most effectively learned. In the following sections we will be addressing some of these issues.

2 The roles of writing

2.1 Differences between writing and speaking

As children learning our mother tongue, we develop, through a process of trial and error, an understanding of the various roles that speaking allows us to assume. We also learn about the sanctions that can be used against us if we use taboo words, and we discover the rewards that we can gain from 'speaking well'. It is usually only in formal education that we come to an understanding of the very different social roles that we can take on if we have access to the written language—for example, recorder of information, researcher, and evaluator of the actions of others. Current descriptions of language by linguists with an interest in its social functions stress that while in speaking the primary emphasis is on the building of relationships, in writing the emphasis is on recording things, on completing tasks, or on developing ideas and arguments. The next tasks investigate these issues. Let us consider first some of the differences between the jobs that written and spoken language do.

 TASK 5

Consider this piece of writing.

---

22 Strathclyde Road
Glasgow GL1A 2AH

The Manager   12th November 1996
Savings Bank PLC
Customer Service Department
Thorpe Wood, Peterborough

Dear Sir or Madam

a/c 9671 06369500

I would be grateful if you could credit the enclosed cheque for £120 (S. Miles 281428 781914 08020068) to my Cheque Account.

I would also be grateful if you could update the passbook for my 60-day Notice Account (9771 04396557) and return it to me at your earliest convenience.

Thank you for your assistance in this matter.

Yours faithfully,

Martin Gordon

Martin Gordon

If you deposited a cheque in person and talked directly to a bank employee about your bank records, would it be appropriate to use the same language forms as those used in this letter? If not, how would the language differ?

In the sorts of spoken exchange that take place in so-called 'service-encounters' in a bank or a shop, the language is very different from that of a formal letter. Here is an example of spoken language used in such an encounter:

M: Can I get cash on a bank card?
C: Do you ... have you got an account here?
M: Not at this branch ... is that a problem?
C: But you bank with ——?
M: Yes, but it's not ... it's in Walthamstow.
C: Can I see?
M: [*inaudible*]
C: That's no problem.
M: Great. Can I have fifty?
C: How do you want it?
M: Tens please.

(*author's transcription of bank service encounter*)

Although the written and spoken texts have certain things in common—a person who wants something done and uses language to get it done—the *types* of language that the speaker and the writer use are different because the social activities are also different. In the written text the distant, formal tone is appropriate for this type of conventional exchange. The writer has never met and will probably never meet the person who processes their request. The communication is one-way and consists to a large extent of neutral formulae. If everything goes well, there will be no need for a reply from the bank; the required transactions will simply be carried out. The shop encounter is a two-way process in which both the customer and the client are necessarily engaged in some kind of personal interaction, and a different type of language behaviour is used to maintain their relationship.

Young children learning to write in a first or foreign language, especially to write formally, can have problems dealing with the sort of one-way communication exemplified above because their main motivation as language learners is to make relationships with other people. Literate adults studying a foreign language will have fewer problems because in most, though not all, cases they have already learned how to write in formal settings. They understand that writing works as a type of discourse, a way of creating a meaningful interaction between the writer and a possible reader. What they may not know, however, is how to use the conventional patterns of organization which are typical of different types of writing in the target language. Nor will they necessarily know how to make appropriate choices from the grammatical and lexical systems on offer to them when they begin to compose texts in a foreign language. As Widdowson says:

> With foreign learners, however, it may be that often the central problem *is* textual rather than discoursal. If the foreign learners have already learnt how to write in their own language, then they will have acquired the essential interactive ability underlying discourse enactment and the ability to record it in text. The problem is how to textualize discourse in a different language.
>
> (*Widdowson 1984:65*)

2.2 Differences between writing and reading

Effectively, everybody learns to speak at least one language fluently, but many are unable to write with confidence. Why should this be so? One of the answers must be that writing normally requires some form of instruction. It is not a skill that is readily picked up by exposure. In this respect, of course, it is like reading, although its social role is very different.

 TASK 6

Think about the things you do between, say, the hours of 7.00 and 9.00 a.m., for example, getting up, having breakfast, and beginning regular tasks inside or outside the home. How many of the things you do would normally involve reading and how many writing?

If you are a commuter, whether getting up in Tokyo or New York, reading is a pervasive requirement: looking at an alarm clock to check the time, glancing at the newspaper, or checking the departures board so you get on the right bus or train. The likelihood that you will spend a lot of time writing during this period is fairly slight. In an industrialized society, reading is a survival skill which enables you to *react* to a range of social demands. Writing, in contrast, is a less necessary skill—but one which can lead to more *proactive* roles.

In Britain in the eighteenth and nineteenth centuries, this was well understood. The argument for emphasizing reading rather than writing in education was (apparently): 'it is desirable that the majority should read—in that way they can be given instructions and can be educated into a particular ideology; writing, on the other hand, assumes the giving of instructions and the *formation* of views about society' (Foggart 1993:6).

Differing abilities to deal with aspects of literacy, for example only being a reader, or being both a reader and a writer, may then be directly linked to the issue of the roles people take on—or have imposed on them—in a particular society. Learning to write is not just a question of developing a set of mechanical 'orthographic' skills; it also involves learning a new set of cognitive and social relations. A version of this view is put thus by Kress: 'Command of writing gives access to certain cognitive, conceptual, social and political arenas. The person who commands both the forms of writing and of speech is therefore constructed in a fundamentally different way from the person who commands the forms of speech alone.' (Kress 1989:46).

To be deprived of the opportunity to learn how to write is, in this view, to be excluded from a wide range of social roles, including those which the majority of people in industrialized societies associate with power and prestige. Similarly, without a capacity to write effectively in the target language, foreign language learners will not have access to roles that would otherwise be available to them, for example in an international community which uses that language for trade or other types of contact.

2.3 Writing and power

If, then, writing is fundamentally an adult activity which is associated with specialized social roles, what exactly are these roles?

 TASK 7

How many of these social activities would you be happy to undertake without doing some writing? Why, or why not?

Inviting three people to dinner
Explaining your child's absence from school
Buying a house
Drawing up the rules of a sports club
Inviting 200 people to a wedding reception
Saying that you are sorry to hear that a friend's parent has died
Shopping in a supermarket
Informing people of the decisions of a committee meeting
Congratulating a friend on a business success
Making a law

All of these activities *could* involve writing. However, some of them demand it if the outcome of the activity is to be successful. For instance, we talk of 'writing' a law, and even the orally presented judgements in a common law system have to be faithfully written down so that they can be worked on by lower courts—or challenged by higher ones. Similarly, although it would be unusual to send written invitations for a dinner party for three close friends, you would be well advised to send written invitations to a wedding reception—and to compile lists of who has been invited and who has agreed to come! Public events which have legal or financial implications are typically dependent on written documentation, and activities which carry with them the need for high levels of systematic organization (for example categorizing) are often more successfully negotiated if writing is used. 'Written language makes a radical difference to the complexity of organization that humans can manage, since it changes the relation between memory and classification, and allows many forms of referencing, cataloguing, indexing, recording and transmitting information' (Stubbs 1987:20–1).

This implies that, for a variety of practical reasons, it is through the mastery of writing that the individual comes to be fully effective in intellectual organization, not only in the management of everyday affairs, but also in the expression of ideas and arguments. 'The mere fact that something is written conveys its own message, for example of permanence and authority. Certain people write and certain things get written' (Stubbs 1987:21). It is for such reasons that writing comes to be associated with status and power. By writing you can have control not only of information but of people.

 # TASK 8

A way of showing the connection between writing, status, and power is to think about how writing is used in organizations. Look at the list of texts below. (1) Which would have to be composed entirely by the writer, and which would most likely be pre-printed forms? (2) Think about three people in a manufacturing company: the Managing Director (MD), a section manager in the Production Department (SM) and a machine operator (MO). Decide which of the following texts are most likely to have been written, or filled in, by which person.

Text	Original text or form?	Who (writes or fills in)?
Safety notice		
Departmental monthly report		
Maintenance report		
Company's annual report		
Letter of dismissal		
Request for time off		
Request for detailed production figures		
Machine breakdown report		

Maintenance reports, requests for time off, and machine breakdown reports are likely to be pre-printed forms which have to be filled in. The other documents are usually original texts. The reasons for this division are very much a function of the uses to which the documents are put and the authority of those who use them. The printed forms are used to communicate upwards, from those in a lower position in a hierarchy to those with managerial responsibility. The information these documents record is needed in a standard and consistent form and requires no creativity on the part of the writer. Indeed, the use of originality and inventiveness would normally be discouraged.

The other documents, those which are not pre-printed forms, are used by managers to get very specific things done. This might either be as a result of the issuing of the document itself (as in the case of a letter of dismissal), or as part of the process of policy formation within an organization. An ability to compose such documents therefore forms part of a manager's repertoire of essential skills.

This discussion has highlighted some of the ways in which learning how to write makes it possible for individuals to take on social roles which are denied to those who do not have this skill. For foreign language learners the picture is more complex. To begin with, they may feel no need to develop a broad repertoire of social roles in the language they are learning. A conversational proficiency, for example, may be all they want. However, if they do decide to extend their range by becoming effective writers in the target language, they should be aware of the issues we have touched on here. When someone learns how to write, they are not just developing a new skill, they are also getting involved in an activity in which questions of social role, power, and the appropriate use of language cannot be avoided.

3 Speaking and writing

3.1 Distinguishing features of spoken and written language

While it is clear that the physical acts of speaking and writing are very different, and while we can see how one language mode might be more appropriate in one social context than another, is it really the case that there are fundamental differences between the language that we use when we speak and when we write?

 TASK 9

Below are four text extracts. Choose the most appropriate places for them on the continuum according to whether they are most likely originally to have been spoken, or written.

written ————————————————————— spoken

Text A
language enrichment /'læŋgwɪdʒ ɪn'rɪtʃmənt/ *n*
a term sometimes used to describe language teaching as part of a programme of COMPENSATORY INSTRUCTION.

Text B
I hope you are both fit and well, I'm managing to keep reasonably healthy, I try to go for two or three outings on my bike each week, when the weather allows.

Text C
OK – in this picture in picture – er – number 1 I can see er a little girl – who probably – is inside – her house – er who is playing – with a bear . . .

Text D
Is the patient work of judges uncovering political corruption and party slush funds hampering French business?

It is probable that you had no difficulty in placing Text A at the 'written' end of the continuum and Text C at the 'spoken' end. Texts B and D present more problems, and you might have put them near the centre. Both these texts have some of the features of language you might think of as 'spoken' along with other features that seem to be typically 'written'. Given our ability to position some texts with a high degree of confidence at either end of this continuum, the question arises as to *how* we distinguish between these extreme examples and why our intermediate examples are more difficult to differentiate. What criteria do we use?

 TASK 10

Are there any features of grammar or vocabulary in your first language that you would find only in written or only in spoken texts?

Contemporary views of the differences between written and spoken language support the idea that they do possess distinctive features and that texts can be distributed along a continuum from the 'most typically spoken' to the 'most typically written'. One reason for investigating these differences is that once students have a better understanding of how spoken and written texts can differ they are much better placed to become confident writers. It is not enough for learners to have a knowledge of the different social roles they adopt when writing or speaking. They also need to see how the different types of language are constructed, and to understand that written texts are not just spoken texts written down.

▶ TASK 11

If possible, record fifteen or twenty seconds of spontaneous conversation and make a transcript, or look at the transcript below. What aspects of the original spoken text do you feel have been lost in the process of transcription?

A: How's Fred going with his pacemaker in his heart?
B: Oh, he's all right.
C: He's all right.
B: He's younger now.
D: Running around; betting like anything.
A: Is he?
D: Cranky as ever.
E: Cranky he is, Alice.
A: Yes.
E: The horse don't win, it's the jockey that's pulled it up, or something – or some other thing.
C: It's all right when it wins though. He only goes crook when they lose.

(recorded by Elaine Daisley, quoted in Halliday 1989:46–7)

Apart from the loss of the contextual information that would have been available to the people in the original conversation—for example, knowledge of the background and the histories of the individuals concerned—two of the most important aspects of speaking that are normally lost in any transcription are prosodic and paralinguistic features. *Prosodic fea-*

tures are the non-verbal aspects of spoken English that are used systematically to help give meaning to utterances: rhythm, phrasing, and pauses being the most important (see pages 50–1 of Dalton and Seidlhofer in this Scheme). *Paralinguistic features* are not a systematic part of the language, but they still add meaning to what we say. These features include the way someone is speaking (for example loudly or softly, shouting or whispering), and the facial expressions and physical gestures they use when they speak. Although handwriting might give us a way of identifying a writer, a transcript of speech loses all of those non-verbal features that identify the speaker as an individual.

Because the writing system cannot directly mimic or represent these non-verbal features of speech, writers have developed ways of compensating for them in cases where their absence would be important. So it is that we use punctuation and other features of typography like bold, underlined, or italicized text.

3.2 Lexical density

One way of looking at written language, then, would be to see it, rather negatively, as spoken language minus certain features. But are there any positive ways in which written language differs from spoken?

 TASK 12

Read the two texts below. What are the most significant differences between them in the areas of grammar and vocabulary?

Text A

L: so suddenly you have to plan your—all your whole day you know

NS: mm

L: and it's all sets up you know you are not very free in a way

NS: have you got into the habit now or is it still hard?

L: well I've got into it now but er then there's problems with the tax people and (blows) you know there's too much things—it's all set down in very little (unfinished)

NS: forms to fill in

(*Faerch and Kasper 1983:151*)

Text B

Purchase price: £72,000

Tenure: Mr Brown is currently waiting for the documented confirmation of his purchase of a share in the freehold owning company and 991 year lease in respect of the above property. This price and transaction have been agreed on the basis that the long lease and share of the freehold is transferred to Mr . . .

Ground Rent: TBA

Service Charge: TBA

Readers of these two passages have commented on the differences in the following terms:

	Spoken	*Written*
Grammar	incomplete utterances	complete sentences
	'incorrect' grammar	complete statements
	hesitation	
	reduced word forms	full word forms
Vocabulary	informal	formal (latinate/polysyllabic)
	phrasal verbs	
	common words	rare words
		conventional abbreviations

The basic grammatical structures of formal written texts are often quite simple; the complexity of the written form would seem to lie principally in the number of content words, or, to put it another way, in the density of the lexis that writers use. In contrast, as Halliday has shown (Halliday 1989), spoken English uses sophisticated and intricate grammatical resources that make conversation and monologue possible.

If we look again at the two examples in Task 12, it should be possible to get a clearer understanding of what is meant by *lexical density*. This can provide an effective means of helping students understand how it is possible for us to put texts in different places on the spoken–written continuum.

▶ **TASK 13**

Consider once more the two examples in Task 12. This time, count the number of grammatical items (for example, articles and prepositions) and the number of lexical items (words that have their own independent meaning) in each.

Text A has a total of 70 words (excluding expressions like 'mm'). Of these, 18 are lexical items ('sets up' and 'set down' have been counted as single lexical items) and 49 are grammatical items ('there's', 'it's', and 'I've' all count as two grammatical items); more than twice as many grammatical words as lexical words. This can be expressed as a lexical density of 26 per cent or 0.26. In Text B this ratio is more or less reversed: it has 63 words, 37 of which are lexical items and 25 grammatical items—a lexical density of 59 per cent or 0.59. This, it appears, is a typical contrast between spoken and written language. 'In general, the more "written" the language being used, the higher will be the proportion of lexical words to the total number of running words in the text' (Halliday 1989: 64).

This simple analysis of lexical density does not, however, give a complete picture of the difference between spoken and written language. We also need to consider whether the lexical items which are counted are common (high frequency) or unusual (low frequency).

   TASK 14

Which of the three statements below seems to be the most characteristic of spoken language?

Text A
Mr Brown is currently waiting for the documented confirmation of his purchase of a share in the freehold owning company. (20 words)

Text B
Mr Brown is now waiting for the papers which will say that he has bought his bit of the company that owns the freehold. (24 words)

Text C
Mr Brown is currently waiting for the documents which will confirm that he has purchased a share in the company that owns the freehold. (24 words)

We have already seen that one of the tests that you might use is to calculate the comparative lexical density of the texts in question. For Text A you would get 20 words / 12 lexical items: ratio = 0.6; for Text B 24 words / 10 lexical items: ratio = 0.41; and for Text C 24 words / 11 lexical items: ratio = 0.46. Nearly everyone who reads these texts says that Text B is the most like spoken language, and the lexical density test would support this intuition—although the ratio is not as low is it would be in many examples of informal conversation. We can also support this claim by looking at differences between the lexical items in Text A and Text B:

Text A
Mr / Brown / currently / waiting / documented / confirmation / purchase / share / freehold / owning / company

Text B
Mr / Brown / now / waiting / papers / say / bought / bit / company / owns / freehold

Text B uses more high frequency than low frequency words: 'now' (versus 'currently'); 'papers' ('documents'); 'say' ('confirm'); 'bought' ('purchased'); 'bit' ('share').

▶ TASK 15

Collect six to ten short samples (of thirty to fifty words) of factual writing from a range of different sources (newspapers, popular journals, academic journals, magazines, school books) and distribute them along a writing–speaking continuum. Then analyse the vocabulary of some of the texts and see if the lexical density/ lexical frequency tests support your intuitive categorization.

This sort of description can help us to see more clearly the specific linguistic contrasts between spoken and written varieties of language, although we can have problems finding individual units of spoken and written extracts that can be truly compared because there are no 'sentences' in spoken language. A refinement of this analysis of spoken–written difference is therefore required to enable us to work with truly comparable samples of language. In a more refined analysis we stop using the written sentence as a unit for comparison. Instead we use the clause as our minimum unit. In this way, we are able to make more meaningful comparisons between spoken and written texts, and can arrive at a more accurate account of lexical density.

▶ TASK 16

Taking two of the examples we worked with in Task 14, how many lexical items are there per clause in texts A and B? (Clause boundaries are shown by two vertical bars ‖.)

Text A
‖Mr Brown is currently waiting for the documented confirmation of his purchase of a share in the freehold owning company‖

Text B
‖Mr Brown is now waiting for the papers ‖which will say ‖that he has bought his bit of the company ‖that owns the freehold ‖

In Text A there is one clause with 11 lexical items. A has a mean lexical density of 11. In text B there are four clauses. The first contains 5 lexical items (Mr / Brown / now / waiting / papers); the second contains 1 (say); the third contains 3 (bought / bit / company); and the fourth 2 (owns / freehold). B then has a mean lexical density of $(5+1+3+2)/4 = 2.75$. This measure of lexical density, combined with an assessment of the relative frequency of the individual lexical items, can provide a reasonably reliable measure for assessing the 'writtenness' or 'spokenness' of different texts.

3.3 Stylistic choice

The above discussion might suggest that we have to write according to a 'lexical density' recipe if our texts are to be accepted as correctly 'written', and that the best writing uses a heavily nominalized style, substituting nouns for verbs in dense clauses like: '. . . his *purchase* of a share in the *freehold owning* company', rather than: '. . . that he has *bought* his bit of the company that *owns* the freehold'. It would, of course, be nonsense to think that this is the case. The theoretical model we have been looking at has dealt with polar extremes. Lexically dense, nominalized styles make it possible to give prominence to certain categories of information and construct a distant impersonal relationship with the reader. Conversational styles of writing which use active verbs in multi-clause sentences achieve completely different effects. Writers in the real world write texts that can be placed at many different points on a continuum between speaking-like and writing-like and we would be very ill-advised to assume that texts can be written to a single strict recipe. In order to do particular 'jobs', writers have to be able to select a style which will best suit context and projected readership. As we saw in 1, the different needs of people engaged in particular social activities have led to the development of writing as a distinctive mode, and the existence of writing has made certain social or intellectual activities possible. Writers, therefore, have had to develop a range of responses to social needs. Some of these involve the use of a heavily nominalized style to ensure that certain categories of key information are given maximum prominence. Others, sometimes as a reaction to the very density and opacity of overly-nominalized styles, tend towards a more conversational tone.

▶ TASK 17

Read the following pieces of writing and think about why the writers have chosen to use writing styles that are more or less conversational.

Text A
Your guarantee
By this Consumer Guarantee, Euro Electronics guarantees this product to be free of defects in materials and workmanship at the time of its original purchase or at the time it was taken on hire purchase terms by the consumer from the retailer for the period of one year.

Text B
Dear Mr Burton,
Now that all our misunderstandings have been cleared up, I feel that it is up to me to make an apology. I apologise to you and Ms Freeman from the bottom of my heart. I only hope that you can accept my sincerity.
Yours sincerely . . .

Text C
A consequence of always proceeding from problems which really are problems—problems which one actually *has*, and has grappled with, is for oneself, that one will be existentially committed to one's work; and for the work itself, that it will have what the Existentialists call 'authenticity'. It will not only be an intellectual interest but an emotional involvement, the meeting of a felt human need.
(*Magee 1973:68*)

The choices that these writers have made are the same ones that we all face when we write something. They involve questions about who the potential reader of the text might be; what effect the writer wants to achieve; what power relationships exist between the addresser and the addressee of the text, and so forth. For one text you might decide that you want to create a sense of maximum distance and neutrality: in another you might want to engage in as direct a contact as possible with your reader.

3.4 Conclusion

An awareness of the differences between the typically written and the typically spoken is essential to writers. An ability to write in a variety of styles—whether it is the informally conversational style of a personal letter, the densely nominalized approach used in some types of academic or legal writing, or something in between—will increase a writer's effectiveness when it comes to addressing different audiences. Gaining an understanding of the linguistic differences between typical written and typical spoken language is an essential part of a writer's education.

Sources of the extracts in Task 9:

Text A – *Richards 1985:157*

Text B – personal communication

Text C – *Bygate 1987:16*

Text D – *Guardian Weekly*, Vol. 151, no 19

4 The organization of written texts

4.1 Introduction

In 3 we saw how typical written language can be distinguished from typical spoken language in terms of lexis and grammar. Here we will shift our focus and consider features of written language that operate above the level of the sentence. In doing this we will look at the organization of written texts from three standpoints. The first relates to the layout, or physical organization on the page, of conventional texts. The second will be concerned with the ways in which texts are organized as a result of the social functions they fulfil. The third considers relationships between clauses and clause complexes within written texts, irrespective of the purpose for which they were written. While many, if not most, competent writers have no conscious awareness of these features of the language, many students learning to write in a second or foreign language have major problems in dealing with them and can benefit from an explicit understanding of how they work.

4.2 Layout

▶ TASK 18

Given below is a simple example of written English which is inappropriately arranged for its particular social purpose. All the words that have been used are correct, but they do not conform to a British reader's expectations for this type of text. What knowledge would you use in order to reorganize the text to make it appropriate to its purpose?

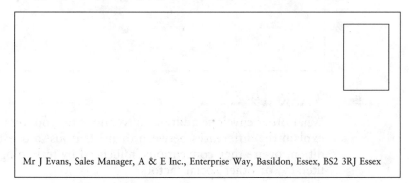

Mr J Evans, Sales Manager, A & E Inc., Enterprise Way, Basildon, Essex, BS2 3RJ Essex

Anyone who is familiar with British letter writing conventions will recognize that this address has been inappropriately organized. In the UK,
normal practice is that such information is presented in a left justified
block about a third of the way from the top of the envelope and about
two inches from the left hand edge. The addressee's name comes first,
followed by their position in their organization (if they are being written to in an official capacity) and then the company, number, street,
town, post code and, if necessary, country.

```
                                                    ┌────────┐
                                                    │        │
                                                    │        │
                                                    │        │
                                                    │        │
     Mr J Evans                                     └────────┘
     Sales Manager
     A & E Inc.
     30 Enterprise Way
     Basildon
     Essex
     BS2 3RJ
     UK
```

This pattern is specific to British addresses and would not be acceptable
in many countries where, for example, address conventions require the
town before the street and the name of the street before the number of
the building.

In Latvia, an envelope might be addressed:

```
                                                    ┌────────┐
                                                    │        │
                                                    │        │
                                                    │        │
     H Sterns                                       └────────┘
     LV 1010, Riga
     Kr Barona 43–16
     Latvija
```

▶   TASK 19

What other envelope address conventions do you know? Can you
explain the differences between them? Is it just a question of tradition, or are they conventions influenced by technology, levels of
literacy, or other social factors?

You could carry out a similar exercise with any other types of highly conventional text, for example a telephone directory or a mail order catalogue. What is important to note here is that a knowledge of how this sort of text is usually arranged in your first language may not guarantee success if you are attempting to write for a different language culture. Telephone directories, mail order catalogues, and envelope addresses are not internationally standardized, even though the functions they fulfil may be almost identical across cultures.

So far, we have done no more than look at the layout of envelopes and how it is determined by different social purposes and technologies (for example, the stamp goes in the top right-hand corner of an envelope because that is where automatic franking machines expect to find it; barcodes are placed in precise locations on envelopes in the US for similar technical reasons). These conventions are relatively simple to teach and to learn how to use. Another question which needs to be considered, however, is whether there are other principles at play which help us to organize the elements *within* a text.

4.3 Social function

One such set of principles has received considerable attention in recent teaching materials. These are related to the concept of *genre*. This term is often used to describe different types of literature, for example lyric, tragedy, novel, or different types of film, for example *film noir*, spaghetti western, musical comedy, and so forth. Educationalists and linguists have recently taken up the concept and used it to refer to language use in specific social contexts. In this context, we can say that genre refers to different types of social activity enacted through different 'texts'—spoken or written—that are associated with them. For example, a sales executive may decide to send a promotional letter to some potential business clients. If the executive understands the genre constraints associated with this sort of writing in a particular cultural context, he or she will not only know about the layout of the genre 'promotional letter', but will also be able to make appropriate lexical, grammatical, and content choices to give the letter the best chance of success with this type of reader. The executive, the letter, and the potential clients are all participants in the genre, each having a role to play. If the executive has done his or her research correctly, has enough understanding of the genre to use it effectively, and has the linguistic skill to word the letter persuasively, there is a good chance that it will do the desired job and sales will be made.

▶ TASK 20

The three texts below are all typical of a particular genre in business writing. What is it? What linguistic clues helped you to identify the managerial/administrative task these letters fulfil?

Letter A

```
                                         QMF
                                         213 Highlands Building
                                         Kowloon
                                         Hong Kong

Ms Emily Wu                              24 June 1995
Apt 20 Folton Heights, Lantau
Hong Kong

Dear Ms Wu

Many thanks for coming to for interview on Friday
afternoon. I was enormously impressed by your enthusiasm,
professionalism and commitment to your work. I knew the
decision I would have to take would be difficult-and it has
been. However, I have made that decision, and I am afraid that I
have not selected you for this particular training programme.

I do hope that you will keep in touch with QMF and that you
can take advantage of future training opportunities.

Thank you again for coming for interview.

Yours sincerely

EJ Choi

EJ Choi
Training Director, QMF
```

Letter B

```
                                         The JGW Foundation
                                         18 Victoria Gardens
                                         Sydney NSW 2305
24 June 1995                             Australia
Mr Colin McInnes
43 Dreadnought St
Bradford, UK

Dear Mr McInnes

Thank you for your enquiry about funding for a Computer
Science course. Unfortunately, I regret we are not in a
position to help you at the moment

You might be interested to know, however, that the
Foundation does have a programme of scholarships and
exchanges in areas such a Economics, Law, Business, and
Computer Studies. I am afraid that we have already
completed the selection for this year, but we will be
inviting applications for next year some time in the Autumn.

All best wishes

A.N. Wisden

A.N. Wisden
Funding Committee Secretary
```

Letter C

```
                                        The JGW Foundation
                                        18 Victoria Gardens
                                        Sydney NSW 2305
         24 June 1995                    Australia


         Dr Anne Porter
         16a Coleridge Road
         Perth
         Western Australia

         Dear Dr Porter

         I am writing to thank you for the interest you have shown in
         the JGW Foundation Seminar on Literary Linguistics. There
         have been over 120 applications to attend the seminar, but
         I am afraid that only a limited amount of space is
         available. In order to implement a fair system of
         allocation, this time we have given priority to
         participants who registered early.

         I am, therefore, sorry to disappoint you and to say that we
         will not be able to offer you a place at the Literary
         Linguistics seminar. We will be keeping your application on
         our files and I can assure you that you will be given
         priority in future registration for our forthcoming
         conferences. I would also like to remind you about our next
         conference on Computers, Writers and Texts (February 1996).
         Do please contact the Foundation if you would like to have
         further details and registration forms for this important
         event.

         Thank you again for your interest

         Yours sincerely
              G. W. Sullivan
         GW Sullivan (Ms)
         Seminars and Conferences Secretary
```

Each of these letters is in some sense rejecting the recipient. We can recognize this from certain key lexis, for example, the expression 'I am afraid' occurs in all three letters, and also from the way in which each letter:

- initially acknowledges the recipient as a person with needs and feelings
- attempts to give some reason for the rejection
- attempts to maintain a friendly relationship with the rejected person.

Such texts are typical of the rejection letters written by cultural and grant awarding organizations, and form a distinct genre.

It should be now clear that, as writers, we need to know:

– what grammatical and lexical choices need to be made in order to match the text to the writing purpose
– how to organize texts appropriately to do particular jobs
– how to recognize the genre in which we are writing.

In 6 we will consider in more detail some of the ways in which a genre approach to writing can be useful for teaching.

4.4 Clause relations

The third aspect of text organization which we will consider now draws on our experience of how languages in general—and English in particular—operate. Here, we shall not be so concerned with particular genres and the social relationships in which the texts which belong to them are involved. Rather we will be looking in more general terms at how language is used to make connections within written texts of all kinds.

▶   TASK 21

Study the following sentences and rewrite the passage in what you feel to be the most logical order. The sentences have been numbered for convenience.

A comparison of two national approaches to the problem of icy roads

(1) In England, however, the tungsten-tipped spikes would tear the thin tarmac surfaces of our roads to pieces as soon as the protective layer of snow or ice melted. (2) Road maintenance crews try to reduce the danger of skidding by scattering sand upon the road surfaces. (3) We therefore have to settle for the method described above as the lesser of two evils. (4) Their spikes grip the icy surfaces and enable the motorist to corner safely where non-spiked tyres would be disastrous. (5) Its main drawback is that if there are fresh snowfalls, the whole process has to be repeated, and if the snowfalls continue, it becomes increasingly ineffective in providing some kind of grip for tyres. (6) These tyres prevent most skidding and are effective in the extreme weather conditions as long as the roads are regularly cleared of loose snow. (7) Such a measure is generally adequate for our very brief snowfalls. (8) Whenever there is snow in England, some of the country roads may have black ice. (9) In Norway, where there may be snow and ice for seven months of the year, the law requires that all cars be fitted with special steel-spiked tyres. (10) Motorists coming suddenly upon stretches of black ice may find themselves skidding off the road.

(*Winter 1976, quoted in Hoey 1983:4*)

In arriving at a solution to this particular problem (the original text is on pages 35–6), you will have used very different sorts of knowledge from that required in Tasks 18, 19, and 20. In those you were able to draw on your knowledge of the typical layout and organization of certain texts with specific social functions. In this last task, it has been necessary to draw on your knowledge of how texts are structured internally. The text organization here is not so specifically associated with a particular social context as are the features of the letters of rejection, but with a set of typical textual patterns which competent readers can recognize because they are signalled by specific lexical markers (for example *first*, *next*, and *then*, or phrases like *the problem is* . . . or *on the other hand* . . .), or because readers are familiar with the usual stages of development of a wide range of different text types.

Texts which are linked by the kinds of lexical markers mentioned above can be described as *cohesive*. One way of seeing how as writers we produce cohesive texts—and how as readers we make sense of texts—is to play 'Serious consequences', which is based on the party game of 'Consequences'. (In this game, the players take turns to write a sentence on a sheet of paper which is then folded over and passed on to the next player so that he or she cannot see what has been written. A nonsense text is produced, which can be very amusing.) In 'Serious consequences' you are allowed to see the sentence which immediately precedes the one you have to write. When it is your turn to write, you must avoid being irrelevant, and should try to make what you write follow on as appropriately and logically as possible from what your immediate predecessor wrote.

▶ TASK 22

> If you are working in a group, try playing 'Serious consequences'. Given below is a sample starting sentence taken from a textbook on computer programming. Try working with this sentence:
>
> 'The best way to program is to think and write in a notation as *abstract as possible*.'

An example of a text which resulted from this game is given below:

1 The best way to program is to think and write in a notation *as abstract as possible*.
2 If this general rule is followed, the programs that are produced are likely to be successful and to achieve the results that you hope for.
3 Beware, however, of the temptation to run before you can walk!
4 Such over-ambition can only lead to disaster of one form or another.
5 On the other hand, the spirit of experimentation should never be entirely quashed.

6 Without it we would never have achieved those few things of which we can be truly proud—the work of a da Vinci, the great city in the jungle at Angkor Wat, the first steps on the Moon or the eternal Pyramids.

The sentences are linked together in a sequence, so we have a text which is cohesive. *Cohesion* is achieved through the use of pronouns and reference words, lexical repetitions, and other logical markers. But the sequence of sentences does not result in any structured argument. The text does not seem to be going anywhere. In this respect it lacks *coherence*. This is not surprising, of course, since it is not under the control of a single writer.

As readers, our first tendency on beginning to read any piece of writing is to assume that it has something to communicate, and we immediately set off to make sense of the text—in other words, to make it *coherent*. If the text displays formal linking devices (in the example above, referring expressions such as '*this* general rule', '*such* over-ambition'; and discourse markers like *however* and *on the other hand*) we assume that they are there to organize the sentences into a larger structure. In the example, however, these devices only serve to stick sentences together in a sequence. The text is not coherent because it is without purpose. It has no overall structure. It describes nothing, it develops no arguments, and hence, in spite of our best efforts, whatever sense we make of it is fairly restricted.

This is not to say, however, that 'Serious consequences' always produces unacceptable texts. In Task 23, a sentence from a novel has been used as a starting point. Groups working with this sentence consistently produce a different kind of text from the kind which results from the sentence in Task 22.

▶ **TASK 23**

Play 'Serious consequences' again, this time using the text below:

'By one-thirty I had driven the twelve miles to San Luis Obispo and I was still circling through the down-town area, trying to orient myself and get a feel for the place.'

It is probable that this time, you will have produced a more acceptable text than the one which resulted from the 'programming' sentence. This is borne out by the results that groups of students have come up with. An example is given below:

1 By one-thirty I had driven the twelve miles to San Luis Obispo and I was still circling through the down-town area, trying to orient myself and get a feel for the place.

2 I decided to park my car outside a small hotel with a broken neon
  sign which flashed 'Wel . . .' at unpredictable intervals and gave a
  greenish cast to the faces of people on the sidewalk.
3 I looked around me carefully before opening the door and getting out.
4 The first thing that I noticed once I was out was that the temperature must have been well below freezing.
5 I wished I hadn't left my gloves in the house.
6 Without them I was going to have problems handling the falcon—it
  had talons like needles—and I had nothing with me to protect my
  hands.
7 The twins knew more about falconry than I would ever know and I
  was sorely in need of their help.

How the story would develop over a longer span is of course uncertain,
but within the limits of the game, the text is a great deal more acceptable than the 'programming' example above. An explanation for this
could be that the expectations readers have of a narrative are much less
problematic to meet than those of a technical or philosophical text. In
fiction, the writer must produce something convincing enough to engage
the reader's interest—but this can be stretched a long way. For example, we may have a slight problem in accepting that the temperature is
below freezing in what sounds like a Southern Californian setting, but
a major part of our pleasure when we start to read a novel or story is
that we cannot predict what content will follow and, hence, we are willing to cooperate with the writer in making sense of the tale. With the
technical text we have different expectations and require it to develop
in more predictable ways if we are to be satisfied as readers.

From this discussion it would seem that a simple enumeration of examples of the linguistic features associated with text cohesion cannot solve
the problems of coherence highlighted in the examples above (see also
pages 127–33 of Cook: *Discourse* published in this Scheme). We can
see, however, that the idea of genre can be drawn upon to explain the
relative acceptability of the narrative text as opposed to the unaccept-
ability of the technical one. The reader expectations that are set up by
a narrative are so open that even a multi-author game can produce quite
satisfactory texts—our expectations cannot be disappointed when part
of the pleasure of a story is the unexpectedness of its outcomes. By contrast, the technical text fails precisely because as an example of a particular genre it creates expectations of a certain type of coherent
development.

One way to test the coherence of a written text (and also to appreciate
how coherence is maintained across a text) is to treat it as if it were in
fact one half of a dialogue (see Hoey 1983, Widdowson 1983). The idea
here is that each sentence of a text is a remark made by the writer which
anticipates a reaction from the reader. The imagined reaction is then
responded to by the writer's next sentence. For example, Widdowson
1983, quotes a text from Gombrich's *Art and Illusion*:

The Greek revolution deserves its fame. It is unique in the annals of mankind. What makes it unique is precisely the directed efforts, the continued and systematic modifications of the schematic of conceptual art, till making was replaced by the matching of reality through the new skill of mimesis.

and shows how the following dialogue can be derived from it:

The Greek revolution deserves its fame.
Why?
It is unique in the annals of mankind.
In what way unique?
What makes it unique is precisely the directed efforts, the continued and systematic modifications of the schematic of conceptual art, till making was replaced by the matching of reality through the new skill of mimesis.

(*Widdowson 1983:60*)

▶ **TASK 24**

Now carry out your own reconstruction of the dialogue which is presupposed in the following narrative text. Note how the writer creates curiosity to find out what will happen next, or an explanation for why events have taken place.

Suddenly she came upon a little three-legged table, all made of solid glass: there was nothing on it but a tiny golden key, and Alice's first idea was that this might belong to one of the doors of the hall;
?
but, alas! either the locks were too large, or the key was too small, but at any rate it would not open any of them.
?
However, on the second time round, she came upon a low curtain she had not noticed before, and behind it was a little door about fifteen inches high:
?
she tried the little golden key in the lock, and to her great delight it fitted!
?
Alice opened the door
?
and found that it led into a small passage, not much larger than a rat-hole:
?
she knelt down and looked along the passage into the loveliest garden you ever saw.
?

(Lewis Carroll: *Alice's Adventures in Wonderland*)

The implications of this view of writing—and its interpretation—are summarized by Hoey:

> The writer initiates his discourse with a first sentence. ... The reader scans the first sentence and forms expectations as to the information that might follow. No harm is done by representing these expectations as questions. The writer then offers a further sentence as an answer to one or more of his or her questions (or expectations). If something in the sentence signals that the question being answered is not one on the reader's short list, then the reader retrospectively has to re-create the question that it must be answering, and if this is in turn impossible, the reader assumes that the sentences are in fact unrelated and seeks a relation elsewhere in the discourse.
>
> (*Hoey 1983: 170–1*)

4.5 Discourse relations

Hoey's reference to 'a relation elsewhere in the discourse' introduces the next stage in our own discussion, as it implies that in addition to the implicit dialogue we have just discussed, there are also larger structures which are not directly expressed by the sequence of sentences in a text—some underlying principle of ordering which supports coherence. One such principle is to be found in what Hoey calls 'discourse relations'.

 TASK 25

Consider the following sentences. They can be combined in twenty-four different ways. Which do you feel is the most probable sequence?

I opened fire.
I was on sentry duty.
I beat off the attack.
I saw the enemy approaching.
(*Hoey 1983:35*)

Of the twenty-four combinations, the one which is accepted by most people who attempt the task reads:

I was on sentry duty.
I saw the enemy approaching.
I opened fire.
I beat off the attack.

It is this version that could be described as the neutral unmarked version. The question arises as to why it is this order which is generally preferred. One explanation which can be offered is based on the notion of *schema* (plural *schemata*), which can be described as a generally accepted way of organizing ideas which provides a basis for readers' expectations of how a text will develop (see Cook: *Discourse* pages 68—74). In this view of language in use, not only do we have expectations of the relationships which words have within sentences, and which sentences have in sequences, but we also have knowledge of how information is organized in the real world which helps us to solve problems like that posed by the text in Task 25. In the case of that example, Hoey suggests we associate the sentences with elements of the general schema: SITUATION — PROBLEM — SOLUTION/RESPONSE — EVALUATION/RESULT.

The underlying schematic pattern of a text can be left implicit, as is often the case in unambiguous contexts. It can also be made explicit by lexical signalling. Thus we can 'spell out' the pattern of the 'sentry text' in the following way:

'*The situation was that* I was on sentry duty and *a problem arose*: I saw the enemy approaching . . .'

Writers can make the *discourse relations* of texts—that is the way their different parts relate to one another—either more or less explicit. In this way, they are able to control the amount of support that they give readers. In some cases they may let the text 'speak for itself' and let the readers' schematic knowledge of discourse help them navigate their way through it. In situations where there is a risk that the reader will not interpret the text in the way the writer wants, it is possible to direct their interpretation by means of explicit lexical signals.

The usefulness of an understanding of discourse relations can best be seen when things go wrong. Consider the following example of the problems which can occur when a writer fails to signal clause relationships with sufficient explicitness.

> A 'breathalyser' indicates the amount of alcohol in a person's body, rather than his reaction to alcohol. Dr Donald E. Sussman has developed a device which measures the unsteadiness of a drinker's eyes—just one of the neurophysiological effects of drinking. [*The remainder of the discourse describes the device and preliminary tests.*]

(*New Scientist*, March 1970)

In this text we are faced with the problem of an opening sentence which does not seem to be connected with the statements which follow. In the implicit dialogue between writer and reader this first sentence sets up the question: 'HOW do breathalysers do this?' But the following sentence does not answer this question. In their discussion of this passage, Hoey and Winter (1986) demonstrate that the reader's interpretative problems stem from the fact that the writer wanted to establish a PROBLEM — SOLUTION pattern, but failed to do so. They propose the introduction of the signal word 'problem' as in: 'The problem with the breathalyser is that it only measures the amount . . .' as a way of eliminating this difficulty.

The schematic pattern of SITUATION — PROBLEM — SOLUTION/ RESPONSE — EVALUATION/RESULT is one of several sets of discourse relations which can be identified, each providing an interpretative framework for readers of texts and a productive framework for writers. Examples of others include REASON—RESULT, and GENERAL—PARTICULAR. But how do schemata relate to the specific genres (for example, rejection letters) discussed earlier?

This connection can be made clearer if we think of two broad sets of schemata as being in play in the development of a specific genre. The first set is associated with the world of 'second person' relationships, in other words how 'I' relates to 'you'. Such second-person schemata are drawn upon when we set the level of formality of a spoken or written text, or as we develop an argument. A failure to make appropriate use of these schemata can result in communication breakdowns if an inappropriate level of formality makes the person addressed feel patronized or insulted, or if the reader is confused because she or he cannot make sense of an argument, as in the case above.

The other set of schemata can be thought of as 'third person' schemata, in other words how 'I' relates to 'he', 'she', or 'it'. These help us to develop physical and conceptual relationships with the world around us. For example these schemata are drawn upon in making the connection between words like 'alcohol', 'drinker', and 'neurophysiological' in the example above.

What happens in the formation of conventional genres is that the use of certain second or third person schemata becomes more or less fixed, so that, for example, as experienced readers of English, we are able to recognize a letter of rejection or a letter offering a job within the first couple of lines. If these schematic routines are not known to a reader, or not exploited by a writer, a text cannot be matched with a specific genre and a much greater processing load is thrown on the reader.

4.6 Conclusion

In 4 we have considered a range of conventions which characterize the activity of writing: conventions which have to do with the relatively simple matter of layout, but also with accepted ways of organizing thought and formulating intention. We have also considered how these discourse conventions are given expression in the process of enacting a relationship between writer and reader. Learning to write implies both an understanding of these conventions and an ability to put them into practice.

Original text for Task 21:

A comparison of two national approaches to the problem of icy roads

(8) Whenever there is snow in England, some of the country roads may have black ice. (10) Motorists coming suddenly upon stretches of black

ice may find themselves skidding off the road. (2) Road maintenance crews try to reduce the danger of skidding by scattering sand upon the road surfaces. (7) Such a measure is generally adequate for our very brief snowfalls. (5) Its main drawback is that if there are fresh snowfalls, the whole process has to be repeated, and if the snowfalls continue, it becomes increasingly ineffective in providing some kind of grip for tyres. (9) In Norway, where there may be snow and ice for nearly seven months of the year, the law requires that all cars be fitted with special steel-spiked tyres. (6) These tyres prevent most skidding and are effective in the extreme weather conditions as long as the roads are regularly cleared of loose snow. (4) Their spikes grip the icy surfaces and enable the motorist to corner safely where non-spiked tyres would be disastrous. (1) In England, however, the tungsten-tipped spikes would tear the thin tarmac surfaces of our roads to pieces as soon as the protective layer of snow or ice melted. (3) We therefore have to settle for the method described above as the lesser of two evils.

5 Approaches to the teaching of writing: process

5.1 Introduction

The teaching of writing has long been a central element in all educational systems, and there are many, often conflicting, views of the best ways of going about it. We might identify three principal ways of approaching the task: focus on form, focus on the writer, and focus on the reader (see Raimes, 1993: 237-60). These three perspectives inform three major movements in the teaching of writing. The first is a traditional, text-based approach which is still used in many materials—as we will see in Section Two of this book. Teachers who focus on form often present authoritative texts for students to imitate or adapt and so are likely to use textbooks which give a good range of models. They will also tend to see errors as something that they have a professional obligation to correct and, where possible, eliminate. In such a context, one of the teacher's main roles will be to instil notions of correctness and conformity.The second approach, which we will explore in the rest of 5, has developed in part as a reaction against this tradition and focuses on the writer as an independent producer of texts. It lays particular stress on a cycle of writing activities which move learners from the generation of ideas and the collection of data through to the 'publication' of a finished text. Because of this emphasis, this newly emerging approach has often been called the *process approach* to teaching writing skills. The third approach is more socially oriented and focuses on the ways in which writers and texts need to interact with readers. In this approach, writing is seen as an essentially social activity in which texts are written to do things, the assumption being that if the reader cannot recognize the purpose of a text, communication will not be successful. This focus on the reader has come to be associated with what are often called *genre approaches* to writing, which we will explore in 6.

5.2 Models of the writing process

Teachers who have been at the forefront of the development of the process approach have proposed methodologies which emphasize the creativity and unpredictability of writing. They have been aided by a significant body of research which has examined what happens while writers write, and has thereby contributed to our understanding of the processes of writing. The process approach has had such a widespread influence on the teaching of writing throughout the English speaking world (see, for example: Zamel 1983; Raimes 1985,1993; White and Arndt 1991) that it needs to be considered in some detail.

 ## TASK 26

Think about the last piece of extended writing you did in your first language or in a foreign language (i.e. more than three or four pages), or talk with a colleague and find out about something they have written. Consider the various stages which had to be gone through order to get the text into an appropriate state to be made public (for example, presented to a management committee, handed in to an academic supervisor, or sent to a journal for publication.)

The stages outlined in Figure 1 are among the most commonly reported.

PREWRITING
(specifying the task / planning and outlining / collecting data / making notes)

↓

COMPOSING

↓

REVISING
(reorganizing / shifting emphasis / focusing information and style for your readership)

↓

EDITING
(checking grammar / lexis / surface features, for example punctuation, spelling, layout, quotation conventions, references)

Figure 1

Simple linear models of the writing process have, however, been criticized by a number of teachers and researchers as not giving a full picture of what successful writers actually do (see Zamel 1983; Raimes 1985). They have described the process of writing as recursive and complex. In other words, although there are identifiable stages in the composition of most extended texts, typically writers will revisit some of these stages many times before a text is complete.

TASK 27

Think again about the process of composing an extended piece of writing. Design a 'flow-chart' or diagram which represents your own understanding of the processes you find yourself involved in when writing. While it may be easy to think of a linear progression as you read from 0 to 4,000 words, it may be more difficult to visualize what happens in the process of writing the same specific text.

It is probable that you found that the different stages appeared more than once, and in different sequences. It is clear that the linear simplicity of the model in Figure 1 has to give way to something more convoluted, more complex. This can be represented by Figure 2, which shows the whole process not as a fixed sequence but as a dynamic and unpredictable process.

Figure 2

This process has been described as follows:

> Contrary to what many textbooks advise, writers do not follow a neat sequence of planning, organizing, writing and then revising. For while a writer's product—the finished essay, story or novel—is presented in lines, the process that produces it is not linear at all. Instead, it is recursive . . .
> (*Raimes 1985:229*)

By 'recursive', Raimes means that at any point in the preparation of a text, writers can loop backwards or forwards to whichever of the activities involved in text composition they may find useful. This could mean that when a writer is a short way into the task, they may find it necessary to go back to the library to collect data, the need for which was not apparent at the planning stage. The writer may then need to revise the plan radically in order to cope with changes that have developed in the argument, or may want to revise the style of earlier sections before going on to write later parts of the text as they come to appreciate how best to reach their intended audience.

5.3 Protocols

Such a model of what happens when successful writers write has been established through direct research into what writers actually do while composing. Using *protocols* (audio recordings of writers who volunteer to 'think aloud' about their mental processes while they are writing) researchers into the practices of expert and apprentice writers, in first or foreign language settings, have established a considerable level of agreement as to what they feel is involved in the production of a successful piece of writing. This research has also caused them to call into question basic assumptions about how to teach students to write—again, both in first and foreign language settings. You can get an idea of the sort of data these researchers have worked with by finding out about how other writers write.

▶ TASK 28

Either record your own thoughts or ask one or two colleagues or students (who you think are good writers) to record their own thoughts as they complete the following writing task. Compare the different stages and activities that each writer uses.

Writing task: You want to sell a flat or house that you have lived in. Write a short description (no more than half a page) in your first language, or a foreign language that you know well, which you could give to people who were interested in buying it. You have a maximum of fifteen minutes.

Instructions: Record your / the writer's thoughts. An example protocol is given below. The words in italics are the transcription of the writer thinking aloud; the words in bold are the actual text that was written.

'I'm thinking about a house I lived in in Nancy . . . what sort of things will people want to know ? . . . **This beautiful** *. . . is "beautiful" the right word? Yes, I think so. . . .* **house in a quiet street near to the centre of Nancy** *. . . is it "near to" or "near"? I think it's just "near". I need to make a list of the best things about it . . . I can select the things that will help it sell . . .'*

The focus on the writer inherent in the development of process approaches has brought a range of benefits to teachers and students. Teaching and learning materials which make use of these approaches typically attempt to match writing tasks to the needs of learners and to encourage creativity in very practical ways. A teacher working within such a paradigm will try to respect the learner's cultural background and avoid the imposition of ideas or language behaviour which would deny the validity of his or her own experience. These are positive contributions to writing pedagogy, but this approach has its problems too.

5.4 Problems of the process approach

One problem for teachers who want to use some form of process approach to writing is how to strike a balance between what they feel is important for the development of their students as writers, and the potentially contradictory influence of the teaching materials they often have to work with. For example, a focus on the individual creativity of the writer is in many ways opposed to the behaviourist models implicit in audio-lingual methodology, or even to the Presentation, Practice, Production (PPP) model found in many examples of teaching materials. These paradigms (based on teacher-led approaches to language teaching) were primarily developed to help learners of the spoken language, and emphasize pattern practice, drilling, and the teaching of specific linguistic forms. This has been carried over into much material for the teaching of writing, and can create obstacles for teachers who want to shift the focus of their writing classes.

▶ TASK 29

> Find two or three language teaching textbooks that you have worked with. How many of the activities which focus on teaching writing give students an opportunity to be creative and original from the outset, and how many begin with an example text or texts, or with samples of language that are presented for imitation or incorporation into later exercises?

If one problem for teachers who want to adopt a process approach is the availability of textbooks, another difficulty is how to assess whether a process approach is applicable in all settings where writing is taught. As this approach focuses primarily on the writer 'as originator of written text' in a context where 'the *process* through which the writer goes to create and produce discourse is the most important component in the theory' (Johns 1990:25), it has proved helpful for many teachers and students in college education—in the USA for example. In this context, a large part of the thrust towards process approaches to writing came from a desire to escape from prescriptive 'modelling' approaches to academic writing. As one writing teacher reports:

> I, like so many of my students, was reproducing acceptable truths, imitating the gestures and rituals of the academy, not having confidence enough in my own ideas, not trusting the native language I had learned. I had surrendered my authority to someone else, to those other authorial voices.
>
> (*Sommers 1992:28*)

Here, Sommers is voicing her negative experience of the first-language writing instruction she received in college academic writing classes, and is searching for a new response to students' needs.

It is difficult to argue against an approach which has as its objective the production of students who 'not only have a large repertoire of powerful strategies, but . . . sufficient self-awareness of their own process to draw on these alternative techniques as they need them. In other words, they guide their own creative process.' (Flower 1985: 370: quoted in Johns 1990: 26). This is shown by the comments of the college grade students at the beginning of their careers quoted below:

> 'At the beginning I have some order in mind, but I don't really know what's going to happen.'
> 'I don't know how it's going to come out. I know what I basically want to do, but I don't know exactly what I'm going to say.'
> 'Unless you write about something, you can't find exactly what you know about.'
> (*Zamel 1983:176*)

These students appear to see their development as writers in terms of their development as thinkers. For them, learning to write, as we have seen in earlier sections in this book, is associated with learning different ways of dealing with the world. However, this is not necessarily representative of the situation in which all writing students find themselves, especially those learning to write in a second or foreign language.

▶ ## TASK 30

Much process-approach theory has been developed in order to address the needs of native speaker and ESL college composition students in the USA. What differences are there likely to be between these students' writing purposes and those of, for example, adults learning to write in a foreign language for professional purposes?

Many adult learners come to the foreign-language classroom with fully developed competencies as writers in their first language. The most appropriate programme of study for such learners will differ radically from the type of writing course needed by 18-year-old undergraduates who may not yet have learned to write effectively even in their first language. It may be precisely the conventions and constraints needed when writing for a new and unfamiliar readership that the competent adult writer in an foreign-language writing programme is most concerned with. In other words, such students need to know about the genre in which they wish to write. What is more, they usually need rapid access to such knowledge.

5.5 What writers need to know

The range of knowledge that a writer requires when undertaking a specific task can be summarized in the following way:

Content knowledge	Knowledge of the concepts involved in the subject area
Context knowledge	Knowledge of the context in which the text will be read
Language system knowledge	Knowledge of those aspects of the language system necessary for the completion of the task
Writing process knowledge	Knowledge of the most appropriate way of preparing for a specific writing task.

▶ TASK 31

Look at the writing assignments below. What kinds of knowledge would a writer need in order to complete each one satisfactorily? Using the four categories of knowledge given above, estimate the relative proportions of each type of knowledge that might be required for the completion of each assignment, for example 30% content knowledge, 25% writing process knowledge, etc.

1 Prepare an internal company report evaluating a newly introduced office automation strategy.

2 Write an examination essay with the title 'Capital punishment is the only answer to the problem of violent crime'.

3 Write a product description brochure for a new range of acrylic automobile paints.

4 Write an M.Sc dissertation in a university department of aeronautical engineering where English is the medium of instruction and assessment.

What follows is an example response for assignment 1. The group who prepared it felt that the most important knowledge that was needed would be about the topic itself—*content knowledge*. Without this, the writer could not prepare an effective report. They also felt that it would be very important for the writer to be aware of power relationships within the company if they were going to be successful in preparing a persuasive document: they would need *context knowledge*. Equally important, the writer would need *language system knowledge*—and not just the specialist lexis of the field, but also knowledge of the grammatical resources of the language so that the report would be written in such a way that it would match the expectations of its readership. The smallest proportion in this instance was *writing process knowledge*. The group felt that while this was clearly important, the other elements were likely to be more significant.

Content knowledge	35%
Context knowledge	25%
Language system knowledge	25%
Writing process knowledge	15%

So far as the other assignments were concerned, assignment 2 (the examination essay question) was felt to be the one which needed most writing process knowledge. This is an interesting conclusion as this task is the one most closely associated with language learning classrooms and is, in many ways, 'empty' as a topic. The writer is asked for opinions and ideas, not for a demonstration of technical knowledge. Assignment 3 (the product description brochure) was again felt to need high content and context knowledge. The group felt that assignment 4 (the MSc dissertation) would be the hardest to write as it would need a very high level of *content knowledge*, a very broad understanding of reading and writing *processes*, a full grasp of the conventions and reader / writer relations appropriate to the *context*, as well as a strong command of the *language system*.

If teachers and writers feel that such a wide range of knowledge and experience needs to be brought to bear in order to achieve a satisfactory completion of these writing assignments, it raises questions about the extent to which any one approach to writing instruction is going to meet the needs of learners. This issue will be addressed in 6.

5.6 Conclusion

In 5 we have looked at how research into what people do when they write has led to the development of an approach which focuses on the processes involved in writing rather than the more traditional emphasis on the use of written products as models, a practice common in many educational systems and language learning materials. Much of the value of process writing has derived from its invigorating effect on classroom writing practices and from its recognition of the importance of the experiences that learners bring with them to the classroom. However, it has its limitations and cannot be seen as answering the needs of all types of student.

6 Approaches to the teaching of writing: genre

6.1 Introduction

In 5, we considered approaches to the teaching of writing which focus on the writer and give special emphasis to the processes involved in writing. A question which arose in this discussion was the extent to which a methodology with a primary focus on the writer can fully address the needs of all learners, especially if they are learning to write in a second or foreign language. While a process approach will certainly make it possible for apprentice writers to become more effective at generating texts, this may be of little avail if they are not aware of what their readers expect to find in those texts:

An example of the sort of problem which can arise when writers do not have a full sense of what their reader expects from a text is explored in the next task.

▶ TASK 32

Both of the texts reproduced below were written by intermediate level students of English (Cambridge First Certificate candidates). Although neither is a model 'letter of complaint', most readers presented with them consider one to be more acceptable than the other. Which letter do you prefer, and why?

Letter A

> Dear Sirs,
>
> After waiting for two weeks for a reply about the letter of complain I send to you. I thought it was necessary for me to write you again in order to let you know how disappointed I am.
>
> My present accommodation is rather ramshackle and moreover I haven't got enough basic facilities, like a real shower with hot water or a toilet flush which is not all the time out of order.
>
> I am expecting from you to something about it as soon as possible, because my conditions of living are rather rough.
>
> I looking forward to hearing from you.
>
> Yours faithfully

Letter B

> Dear Sir,
>
> I am very unhappy with the accommodation you have arranged for me. I have already argued in person but in vain; here the bathroom is dirty and the shower doesn't work and more over a security system is inexistent.
>
> I would like to have a more suitable accommodation.
>
> I look forward to hearing from you.
>
> Yours faithfully

Letter A is usually felt to be more acceptable than Letter B. It is, however, difficult for most readers to explain their decision. Both letters are laid out acceptably and conform to expected opening and closing conventions. Both letters contain vocabulary, spelling and grammar mistakes—indeed, there are more of these in A than in B. Yet Letter A is felt to be better, in spite of its limitations. Understanding why this should be so, and seeing what the implications might be for writing instruction, are two key issues which have not really been addressed by process-oriented approaches, but have been central to those approaches which take as their starting point a focus on the reader.

6.2 Communicative events and communicative purposes

In general, approaches which focus on the reader emphasize the constraints of form and content that have to be recognized when a writer attempts to match a text to a social purpose, and have come to be associated with the notion of *genre*. Our first task will be to come to a clearer understanding of how this term is currently used.

There are various definitions of genre. John Swales (1990) begins an extended definition thus:

Statement 1

A genre comprises a class of communicative events, the members of which share some set of communicative purposes.

(Swales 1990:58)

Swales' definition of genre is a synthesis of contemporary interpretations of the term (see especially Halliday 1989; Kress 1989; Martin 1989) and has contributed to more recent developments in the field of genre studies (see Bhatia 1993). It provides us with a way of looking at language in use which differs in many respects from that inherent in process approaches, but which can complement them. However, interesting as the notion of genre may be, the question remains how such an apparently complex concept can help teachers in the difficult practice of writing instruction.

In the following tasks we will work through all of the statements which make up Swales' complete definition of genre. In doing this it should be possible to make clearer the connection between the focus on the reader typical of this kind of approach and the needs of learners and the writing teacher. Each task will lead to an explanation of the technical terms that Swales uses. The tasks should also make it possible to produce a clearer explanation of why, in Task 32, letter A is preferable to letter B.

In what I have called 'Statement 1' Swales introduces two key terms apart from genre itself: *communicative event* and *communicative purpose*. A communicative event comprises 'not only the discourse itself and its participants, but also the role of that discourse and the environment of its production and reception, including its historical and cultural associations' (Swales 1990: 46), in other words, people using language in an agreed way to get something done. This may involve simple-to-identify classes of text like 'recipe' or, to give a contrasting example, barristers using closed 'yes-no' questions to control how much information hostile or friendly witnesses will be allowed to reveal.

 TASK 33

Each of the communicative events below requires a written text in order to be satisfactorily enacted. In your own language culture, what will be the essential features of each of these texts? How will the historical and cultural associations mentioned by Swales determine the way they are written?

- A company wants to confirm the appointment of a new member of staff.
- A company wants to assure a person buying their product that it will be repaired or replaced if it is faulty.
- A parent wishes to inform a class teacher that their child will be absent from school the following day.

Each of these interactions has a distinct social purpose. As we have seen earlier, the texts that are written to meet the needs of these events, and the people who are engaged in the interaction, are all 'participants' in the event. Thus, unless there is a 'letter of appointment' it may be impossible for employees to prove whether or not they really have a job. In a British company, this letter will name the person to be appointed, and will usually specify the starting date of that appointment. It may also outline the conditions of service and the salary. The letter will frequently contain phrases such as 'I am pleased to inform you . . .', and 'this appointment will commence with effect from . . .', and so on. It will be on paper with the company's letterhead and be signed by an authorized member of staff.

The next event, by contrast, involves a person with legal qualifications, a company, and an unnamed purchaser, and the required text will take on different characteristics. As a legal document, it has to be written by someone with 'expert' qualifications and status. Furthermore, it will contain technically specific vocabulary and turns of phrase that you would not expect to find in other types of document. In some countries it may also require a company seal over the signature in order to attest to its authenticity.

The third communicative event, the letter from a parent to a class teacher, is much less formal but is again recognizable by members of a particular community as a specific type of text. For someone who is a speaker of a different language and who has recently arrived in a community, writing such a letter can present real problems unless they are given advice by other parents or a friendly teacher. Even this simple text will make demands on the writer: the reader will expect certain categories of information to be provided, and the writer will have to take responsibility for maintaining a complex set of relationships between teacher, student, school authorities, and parent.

The term 'communicative purpose' has also been used by Jim Martin (Martin 1989) when describing some of the core genres that schoolchildren need to be aware of as they become writers. Martin discusses various categories of writing done in school: for example REPORT (impersonal account of facts), DESCRIPTION (personal account of imagined or factual events and phenomena, which are largely unchallengeable), RECOUNT (stories about the writer's own experiences), and PROCEDURE (objective accounts of processes taking place in the world around the writer which generalize experience).

▶ **TASK 34**

Martin (1989) quotes an example of a Year 3 Australian school student's writing (Text A) and contrasts it with a re-wording (Text B) which he suggests has another communicative purpose.

Text A
Birds live up in a tree. If they don't eat they die.
Redbirds balckbirds any colored birds. Dark birds light birds.
Some are small and others are big.

Text B
My bird lived up in a tree. It ate so it wouldn't die. It was a black bird and it was small.

(*Martin 1989:7*)

What are the different communicative purposes exemplified here? To which of the four categories mentioned above might these examples belong?

Martin argues that Text A relates to a specific class of social practice—the genre REPORT. The writer is making a general, not a specific statement, and focuses on things rather than events. The important feature of reports is that they can be questioned and then developed through debate without challenging the social identity of the writer or the authenticity of their world view. Text B relates to the genre DESCRIPTION. Here the writer focuses on the specifics of his or her experience rather than on generalities, providing the reader with access to an otherwise unavailable and largely unchallengeable view of the world.

Clearly it is important to give children the opportunity to talk about their own worlds and their own experience. However, it is not helpful to limit students to this single expressive range. Many kinds of writing need to be taught in the school system. As Martin says: '. . . by focusing children's attention on the fundamental differences between DESCRIPTIONS and REPORTS, teachers could help children to learn to write consistently in each genre' (Martin, 1989:7). If such instruction is not given, there is a risk of disabling our students by restricting them to a capacity to express only their own views of the world.

This example shows how wordings—choices available in the grammar and lexis of the written language—change according to the agreed social purpose of a text. It also shows the value of an explicit pedagogic focus on the ways in which contrasting social demands create different genres.

6.3 How genres change

The next statement in Swales' definition provides a further specification of the nature of genre.

> *Statement 2*
>
> A genre comprises a class of communicative events, the members of which share some set of communicative purposes. *These purposes are recognized by the expert members of the parent discourse community and thereby constitute the rationale for the genre.*
>
> (*Swales 1990:58*)

Swales' use of the terms 'expert' and 'parent discourse community' raises the issue of accepted conventions and the extent to which they can be challenged. This can be a problem for teachers who want to focus very strongly on the individual writer as originator of texts and, indeed, raises the whole question of the authority on which conventions are established. Who should have the right to determine the purposes and practices of a discourse community? Can that power be subverted or challenged? The two following tasks look at these issues in a very specific genre.

 **TASK 35**

Read the two text extracts below. What is the genre of which these two texts are examples? What is the communicative purpose that they share as members of this genre?

---

define /dɪˈfaɪn/ **defines, defining, defined**   ♦♦♦◊◊
1 If you **define** something, you show, describe or   VERB
state clearly what it is and what its limits are, or
what it is like. *The Supreme Court decision could*   V wh
define how far Congress can go in trying to deter-   V n
mine the outcome of court cases ... I tried to define
my own attitude: I found Rosie repulsive, but I   ADJ-GRADED:
didn't hate her. ♦**defined** *... a party with a clearly*   usu adv ADJ
defined programme and strict rules of membership.   deliniated
2 If you **define** a word or expression, you explain   VERB
its meaning, for example in a dictionary. *When*   V n
people are asked 'What is intelligence?' they tend to V n asn
reply: 'I don't know how to define it, but I can
certainly recognize it when I see it' ... Collins
English Dictionary defines a workaholic as 'a
person obsessively addicted to work'.

define /dɪˈfaɪn/ *v* **1** ~ **sth(as sth)** to state exactly
the meaning of a word or phrase: [Vn] *Writers of*
dictionaries try to define words as accurately and
clearly as possible. [also Vn-n]. **2** to state or
describe exactly the nature or extent of sth: [Vn]
The powers of a judge are defined by law. [V.wh]
It's hard to define exactly how I felt. **3** to show a
line, a shape, a feature, an outline, etc clearly:
[Vn] *When boundaries between countries are not*
clearly defined, there is usually trouble. ○ *The*
mountain was sharply defined against the
eastern–sky. ▶ **definable** /-əbl/ *adj.*

(*Collins COBUILD English Dictionary* 1995)   (*Oxford Advanced Learner's Dictionary* 1995)

These examples are from the genre 'Dictionary'. Dictionaries have a particular agreed purpose ('a book in which the words of a language are listed alphabetically together with their meanings or their translations in another language'—*Collins COBUILD English Dictionary*; 'a book that gives the words of a language in alphabetical order and explains their meaning, or translates them into another language'—*Oxford Advanced Learner's Dictionary*), and a long tradition which permits a very high degree of stylistic deviation from the wordings of most other written genres, mainly through the extensive use of conventions such as abbreviations, codes, and special typefaces. These conventions are determined by a smaller group of experts, in other words the discourse community of lexicographers.

If we accept that dictionaries have an agreed communicative purpose, that they are immediately identifiable for what they are by general readers / writers, and that the special features of dictionaries are recognizable to members of a discourse community of lexicographers, there are two questions to be answered for the purposes of this discussion. The first is 'How does an educated reader / writer become a lexicographer— a member of that discourse community which writes dictionaries?' The second is 'How do changes in the social activity of dictionary making, and changes in the genre itself, take place?' This second question is important because it is often the case that an individual feels a need to challenge the authority of both seniors and peers and to reinterpret a tradition once they have become a member of a parent discourse community.

In answer to the first question, the main way in which people become lexicographers is by reading different dictionaries and borrowing for new purposes those elements that they find useful in the work of earlier dictionary makers. Although the major dictionary publishers have in-house training programmes for their editorial staff, even this sort of training has, up until very recently, depended on examples of other dictionaries as the principal resource. By and large, people have become lexicographers by means of a close study of the parent genre.

The next task will provide some possible answers to the second question.

▶ TASK 36

Read the examples in Task 35 once more. In several ways, the *COBUILD* example challenges the interpretation of the genre 'Dictionary' in the *Oxford Advanced Learner's Dictionary* example. What is the difference between these two examples of the genre? Why do you think the reinterpretation of the genre has been attempted?

Both examples are members of a special sub-genre of 'Dictionary', i.e. 'Learner's dictionary', which provides a range of information not commonly found in dictionaries for native speakers (for example grammar explanations, information on pronunciation). Both of these dictionaries have been written by expert members of the parent discourse community, but the first example differs markedly from the second. The difference has arisen from a desire to redefine the relationship between the lexicographer (the dictionary writer) and the reader (the dictionary user). As the editor of the *COBUILD* dictionary says: 'This dictionary is written in ordinary, everyday English' (Sinclair et al. 1987: vii). The *COBUILD* dictionary has been widely acclaimed for its 'ordinary language' definitions, and for the way in which it is designed to make information easily accessible to readers. This accounts for the difference between *COBUILD*'s more informal defining style and the more traditional style of the *Oxford Advanced Learner's Dictionary*.

This point is important as it demonstrates how a genre is not a rigid set of rules for text formation. It is social practice, not simply the text, which makes the genre possible, and social practices are open to challenge and change. In the case of the genre 'Learner's dictionary', expert members of that community have reinterpreted a tradition and decided to challenge some of its fundamental premises and practices. As a result, the genre itself has changed. Such genre changes happen all the time, and are a major reason why genre approaches to writing should lead away from prescription. The concept of genre is dynamic, not static, and the student and teacher need to be aware of the fluidity of social practices and the texts which make these practices possible. This awareness has the potential to produce a very different styles of learning and teaching from those associated with approaches which focus on form.

6.4 Reader expectation and schematic structure

Statement 3

A genre comprises a class of communicative events, the members of which share some set of communicative purposes. These purposes are recognized by the expert members of the parent discourse community and thereby constitute the rationale for the genre. *This rationale shapes the schematic structure of the discourse and influences and constrains choice of content and style.*

(Swales 1990:58)

This statement has a bearing on Task 32. We have already seen how the social purposes of a communicative event influence the textual choices that a writer makes. In analysing the problem of the 'letter of complaint' it is now possible to make use of the idea of a genre and to see how—for a British reader at least—Letter A is more happily worded than Letter B. The key seems to lie in the opening of each letter:

Letter A
After waiting for two weeks for a reply about the letter of complain I send to you. I thought it was necessary for me to write you again in order to let you know how disappointed I am.

Letter B
I am very unhappy with the accommodation you have arranged for me. I have already argued in person but in vain; here the bathroom is dirty and the shower doesn't work and more over a security system is inexistent.

Letter A begins with an attempt to establish a relationship with the reader. The writer has recognized that there is a need to explain why the letter is being written, and why he or she feels that there are grounds for complaint. It is only after this attempt at relationship-building has been made that details are given. Letter B, by contrast, goes directly into the detail of the complaint and makes no attempt to establish a relationship with the reader. Even though the writer wants to get something done and to improve the situation, the letter fails to make even the slightest concession to the reader. It would seem that most readers of letters of complaint in English expect there to be this sort of concession. Although 'Letter of complaint' is not a highly technical genre, it does appear to impose constraints on writers who wish to use it effectively and to confer benefits on those who try to conform to those generic constraints. Even if writers do not have full control of the language system, so long as they attempt to signal their willingness to make a relationship with the person they are complaining to—in other words to write within the genre—their letter has a better chance of success. This again indicates how a straightforward focus on form, emphasizing accuracy of expression, will fail to provide learners with the sorts of knowledge that make it possible for them to communicate effectively in given contexts.

This idea of reader expectation relates to the 'schematic structure' which Swales mentions in Statement 3. Swales presents an account of the way in which individuals use their experience of the world to create schemata which they draw on when negotiating meaning in writing. This he represents in the diagram below. In particular, Swales discusses the nature of 'formal schemata' which make it possible for a writer to produce appropriately worded and organized texts for specific social purposes. It is this combination of formal, procedural, and content schemata which makes it possible for us to identify examples of specific genres and to assess their degree of prototypicality (the extent to which an example is seen as being 'centrally' typical of any set). Swales' diagram shows how prior knowledge and experience of the world and of texts combine to produce sets of schemata which determine both the content and form of the texts which are 'allowable' in a particular genre. In the genre 'Letter of complaint', texts which do not attempt to build a relationship with the reader seem to be less allowable than those which do—whatever the grammatical problems in the text.

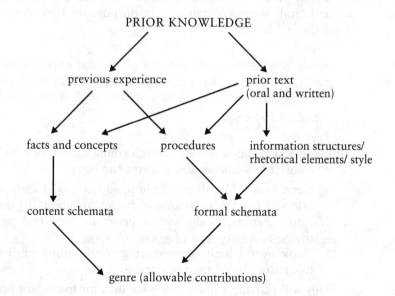

(*Swales 1990:84*)

6.5 Defining typical and less typical examples: communicative purpose

Statement 4

A genre comprises a class of communicative events, the members of which share some set of communicative purposes. These purposes are recognized by the expert members of the parent discourse community, and thereby constitute the rationale for the genre. This rationale shapes the schematic structure of the discourse and influences and constrains choice of content and style. *Communicative purpose is both a privileged criterion and one that operates to keep the scope of a genre as here conceived narrowly focused on comparable rhetorical action. In addition to purpose, exemplars of a genre exhibit various patterns of similarity in terms of structure, style, content and intended audience.'*

(Swales 1990:58)

Statement 4 addresses a problem common to any attempt at categorization: do any particular features have priority over others? While many texts share similar features, for example lexis, typography, and status, for Swales it is the *communicative purpose* of a genre which matters rather than any formal feature. A simple example is given in the following task.

 TASK 37

Decide on a name for the genre in which the following texts might be found. What communicative purpose do they share and how is this achieved?

Text A

Agnès Sorel—Stuff the omelet with minced mushrooms tossed in butter and cohered with thin chicken purée, lay some roundels of tongue on the top, surround with a thread of thickened gravy.

(Saulnier 1914:66)

Text B

Piselli alla Francese—Shell enough young garden peas to fill a two-pint jug. The younger and sweeter the better.

1. Stew, over a low flame, 2 chopped lettuces, 1 chopped onion, salt and pepper, in 10gms of butter for about 10 minutes.
2. Add the peas, along with a generous bunch of parsley and thyme and two cups of good stock.
3. Cook over a high flame stirring continuously until the liquid has reduced and the peas are cooked.

This will provide a main vegetable dish for five or six people. Our cook, Maria, gave it to us for the first time in the early 1950s—she had adapted it from a French recipe she learned during the war.

Our only justification for putting it in a collection of Italian recipes is that we have eaten it so regularly in that part of the world.

Text C

Put your tunny steaks in hot olive oil to brown lightly on each side. Remove, and put aside to keep warm. Now put into your olive oil 2 shallots, chopped; 2 carrots, sliced; a stick of celery, finely chopped, and 4 tomatoes, skinned and chopped. Add a sprig of thyme and cook for 15 minutes. Now put your tunny steaks back into the braising pot, and add wine to cover them. Put the lid on your pan and cook for 1 hour in a slow oven [170°C / 325°F, gas 3].

(Lassalle 1976:177)

It is clear that these texts are all members of a genre called 'Recipe'. Their communicative purpose is to provide the reader with an assured means of producing the dishes that they describe. This requires the writer to provide the reader with, at the least, the following:

– ingredients (usually in fairly precise proportions)
– method
– cooking time and temperature (where relevant)

It is also clear that they are all very different, in spite of having a common communicative purpose which provides us with the means of allocating them to a particular genre. If a teacher is working with students who want to write recipes, it would not be sensible to give these as models for imitation. What texts like these do provide, however, is a resource which can be used for raising students' awareness of the potential forms and wordings of the texts that belong to particular genres. By working in an investigative way, learners can begin to draw some conclusions about what happens in recipes—what stages are frequently found in such texts, what verb forms are most common, how measures of liquids and solids are described —and can then begin to experiment with their own ideas. This sort of investigative work can complement process-oriented approaches to writing to very powerful effect.

Statement 5

A genre comprises a class of communicative events, the members of which share some set of communicative purposes. These purposes are recognized by the expert members of the parent discourse community and thereby constitute the rationale for the genre. This rationale shapes the schematic structure of the discourse and influences and constrains choice of content and style. Communicative purpose is both a privileged criterion and one which operates to keep the scope of a genre as here conceived narrowly focused on comparable rhetorical action. In addition to purpose, exemplars of a genre exhibit various patterns of similarity in terms of structure, style, content and intended audience. *If all high probability expectations are realized, the exemplar will be viewed as prototypical by the parent discourse community. The genre names inherited and produced by discourse communities and imported by others constitute valuable ethnographic communication, but typically need further validation.*

(*Swales 1990:58*)

The last two sentences of Swales' definition state two of the key issues which teachers of writing need to face if they wish to draw on theories about genre when developing programmes of writing instruction. The first is that probability is an essential aspect of genre: in other words, exemplars can be members of a genre to a greater or lesser extent. If all high-probability expectations are realized the exemplar is prototypical of a genre. If not, then the exemplar may occupy a problematic no-man's land.

 ## TASK 38

Continuing with the genre 'Recipe', decide how likely the following texts are to be members of the genre. What criteria would you use for their inclusion or exclusion?

Text A

The influence of the neighbouring region of Emilia Romagna is very evident in the pasta dishes of Tuscany, which ideally should be made from home-made pasta. However, when it comes to the commercially produced dried pasta made from durum wheat, the Tuscan cooks seem to favour spaghetti over all other shapes. I think this has something to do with their innate sense of artistic order—there is something satisfying about a plate of steaming spaghetti.

(*Harris 1992:31*)

Text B

PRESSURE COOKING
Use 15 lb per cubic inch pressure and cook the pulses for about a third of the time given. As the time pulses take to cook can vary, I find, from batch to batch, it's probably best to look at them a little before you think they should be done to make sure. Some of the pulses, particularly the split red lentils and split peas tend to 'froth up' when they come to the boil, and this can clog the valve of the pressure cooker. To avoid this, just add a couple of tablespoons of oil to the cooking water.

(*Elliot 1979:41*)

Text C

Dried mushrooms—If you can find them, Funghi Porcini are the best known (and the most expensive), but you can also find excellent equivalents, often imported from Central Europe. Soak them for two or three hours in hot water or milk and then trim the stems and rinse them (do this carefully as they can be very gritty). Strain the soaking liquid and reserve it, as it can add considerable flavour to sauces and soups. A paper coffee filter is an excellent way of doing this.

In fact, none of the examples given above fulfil the conditions necessary to be prototypically members of the genre 'Recipe'. They either lack the specific purpose of enabling the reader to prepare a particular dish, or the precise detail which we expect of recipes. Text A simply fills in background 'colour' for the reader. Text B gives instructions about a cooking process and has some of the characteristics of a recipe, but not enough to lead readers to feel that it is one. And even Text C, which seems to fulfil most of the conditions, has most information missing: it is a recipe for doing something with mushrooms, but to what end? What do you do with the mushrooms once you have prepared them? Is it a finished dish or must it be added to other ingredients before it is served?

6.6 Genre and social structures

The final sentence of Swales' definition declares that the names of the genres with which a discourse community feels some sense of identity are the source of valuable ethnographic information, *'but typically need further validation'*. The student or teacher of writing who begins to engage in a study of genre will, willy-nilly, be drawn into a study of the social structures which produce the texts; after all, a text is nothing more than a product of the categories of social interactions that are realized by genres. Perhaps the notion of writing instruction needs to give way to an educational paradigm which is more investigative in its orientation.

6.7 Process and genre

We began in 6 with a practical problem: what makes one piece of writing more acceptable than another? It would seem that the notion of genre may provide learners and teachers with a way of tackling this problem. However, while we have discussed genre in some detail, we have not yet considered what a genre approach to the teaching of writing might look like, and how it would differ from the process approach discussed in 5.

While a process approach to writing instruction has many positive aspects, one of its limitations is that it does not necessarily address the needs of a learner who has to write for readers unknown to him or her, especially for readers with specific expectations of what a text should be like if it is to achieve its effect. If we accept that it is helpful for learners in mother tongue and second-language writing classes to develop an ability to express their individual identities through writing *and* to be able to write a broad range of functionally oriented texts—texts which do jobs—in what ways might a genre approach to writing complement the classroom practices which have been developed through process approach methodology?

▶ TASK 39

Consider again the students' letters of complaint which we studied in Task 32. How might a teacher deal with the difficulties which these students were having with writing for a particular genre?

One way of responding to this question is given by Flowerdew (1993). Discussing the needs of learners of English for professional communication, he suggests six types of activity which can help students gain a better understanding of genres in which they have a particular interest. Flowerdew suggests these activities as a way of coping with the fact that genres are not 'clearly delineated constructs, susceptible to rule-governed description.' (Flowerdew, 1993:309). The six activities are:

1 using the results of genre analysis
2 'metacommunicating' (talking about instances of genres)
3 learners doing their own genre analysis
4 concordancing
5 'on-line' genre analysis by learners as an aid to creating their own texts
6 translation based on samples of instances of a given genre

With regard to Flowerdew's first three activities, there are already useful examples of the implementation of this sort of approach. One of the most fully elaborated can be found in Bhatia (1993), where he discusses different ways in which learners can gain important insights from the social, textual, and psychological dimensions of such diverse genres as 'Promotional letters' in business correspondence (Chapter 3), 'Academic writing' (Chapter 4), and 'Legal writing' (Chapter 5). The sorts of analysis he describes involve the learner in a consideration of the social context in which the text is being produced, the role that the text takes in the genre, and the distinguishing linguistic features of the genre, and lead him or her towards production informed by these insights.

The last three of Flowerdew's activities all depend on the availability of a collection of appropriate text examples. In an ideal case this would be a large corpus of computer-readable documents. Great size, however, is not essential. The important thing is that teachers and students should have access to as large a source of authentic data as possible which they can use for research and investigation. The texts need to be representative of the particular genres in which students are interested and should be used as models for discussion and analysis, but not for slavish imitation. Flowerdew makes an interesting point when he comments on modelling: 'Many native speakers make use of others' writing or speech to model their own work in their native language where the genre is unfamiliar. It is time that this skill was brought out of the closet, and exploited as an aid for learning' (1993:313).

What is being advocated is clearly very different from the uncritical imitation of prescribed models. Rather, Flowerdew is recognizing the existence of the process of adoption and adaptation in which all writers participate as they respond to the texts they meet, and is advocating the pedagogic exploitation of such processes. It is important to note that this kind of process is only possible when writers can identify the generic features of particular texts.

The best practical outcome of the approach which Flowerdew proposes is a cycle of activities that can be added to the recursive writing process we have already discussed in 5 (see Figure 2). These activities can provide opportunities for the teacher to draw students' attention to contextual and textual features of genres as part of a language awareness raising programme, or allow students to come to their own conclusions about aspects of text and context.

'Concordancing' is a procedure which has gained currency recently. It refers to a technique in computer analysis common in dictionary making, and is becoming more widely available to language teachers (for a wider discussion of concordancing in language teaching see Tribble and Jones 1989). An example of concordance data from written genres in two different academic fields is given below and illustrates how there can be contrasting uses of the verb 'say' in equivalent genres associated with differing fields. The first sample is taken from the genre 'Journal article' in the field of history, the second from the same genre in the field of engineering science.

```
History

EHR1939    rris. It is a little less than fair to   say that Elisabeth cared more that Essex was
EHR1930    seem to hold? It is a facile answer to    say that Elisabeth ought to have increased her
EHR1930    or so with which we are dealing we can    say that Elisabeth paid out rather more than sh
EHR1970    nationalism in Italy. I am ashamed to     say that for a long time, like many more, I wit
EHR1939    would probably be nearer the truth to     say that he was involved in the less spectacula
EHR1970    his essentially conservative motive: I    say that if Freedom were nothing but a mischiev
EHR1930    iewer might despair of finding much to    say that is new and especially of upsetting any
EHR1988    a private minute, he went so far as to    say that Personally, I think that the jews dese

Engineering

ENGI    mperature. An infinite heat source of,    say, 300 degrees, might be used for the purpose
ENGI    t into contact with a second system B,    say a block of metal, then the two systems are
ENGI    they are insignificant. When analyzing   say a turbine, stage by stage in detail, the ki
ENGI    molecular energy of the element is U,     say, and if the element is moving with a veloci
ENGI    11 points relating to one pressure, pa    say, are joined up to form a constant pressure
ENGI    ample, between states 2 and 3, defined    say by the values p2, v2 and p3, the change
ENGI    g0 Or where the fluid changes phase,      say from saturated liquid f to saturated vapour
ENGI    f a fluid changing phase isothermally,    say from saturated liquid f to saturated vapour
ENGI    ion will not necessarily be TO; let us    say it will be Ti' as in Fig. 7.11a. The work
ENGI    T if each side is equal to a constant,    say K, and hence
ENGI    regarded as steady, the mass flow kgs     say must be constant and the same at inlet and
ENGI    e entropy at state 1, defined by p, v1    say, relative to the entropy at some reference
```

Although this sort of data is most easily obtained with a computer, it is perfectly possible for teachers and learners to use similar techniques in classrooms with little or no technology. Jane Willis (personal communication) reports a procedure she has seen successfully used in classrooms where there was not even an adequate blackboard. Here teachers asked learners to collect examples of particular grammatical forms or lexis during the course of a week, writing each example with a context of six or seven words on each side. These examples were then pinned to the classroom wall, with the 'keyword(s)' positioned in a column—as in the computer example. The insights that learners gain from this sort of procedure are as valuable as those obtained with high technology equipment.

Flowerdew's last activity, translating into and from the target language, depends on the availability of appropriate data from the target language which can be used as a source of information during the process of translation of texts appropriate in one language culture so that they will work in another. Flowerdew discusses the difficulties of translating the abstract of an article on botany from English into French and the need to be aware of a wide range of differences of convention between the genre practices of one discourse community and another.

If we accept that it is important for student writers to be familiar with certain genres, then it is clear that we need to extend the model of writing outlined earlier so as to show how content, context, process, and language knowledge interrelate with each other and can be realized in practical classroom procedures. Figure 3 shows a modified version of the cycle of writing activities we saw in 5.

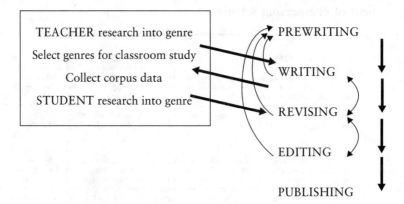

Figure 3

We can see how this interrelationship works by re-visiting the problem posed in Task 39. In this instance, rather than doing pre-writing activities which depended solely on the learners' knowledge of the world, activities can be designed to enhance learners' understanding of the genre in question. The teacher can do some preparatory work on the genre 'Letters of complaint', taking into account the contextual and textual features of the genre. Having done this research, the teacher is in a position to select authentic data both for learners to work with during their own research, and also as a resource which he or she can use to extend his or her own knowledge of the genre. This corpus of texts (paper or electronic) can then become a permanent resource for use in future teaching programmes. The learners can begin their study of the genre either before they start writing, as part of a language awareness raising programme, or they can start off in a process writing cycle and have recourse to genre analysis at moments when they feel a lack of sufficient information regarding the text or context they are addressing. In this way, genre and process approaches become two resources available to learners and teachers.

A recent comment on the debate over the virtues of process and genre approaches to writing summarizes this as follows: 'Unfortunately, the genre/process debate has been typified by false dichotomies and ideological preoccupations. Ultimately, the central issues of freedom and control are not alternatives between which a choice has to be made. They are really interdependent, and effective writing pedagogy will call upon both approaches'
(*Bamforth 1993:97*).

In these terms, it is possible to see the emergence of effective solutions to learning and teaching problems in writing instruction which draw on the strengths of both process and genre approaches, and do not see them as incompatible. In such a paradigm, teachers can provide insights for students that are beyond the learners' own experience; learners, on the other hand, are not totally dependent on the teacher for their knowledge of different genres. By having access to paper or electronic corpus materials which allow for the investigation of how texts work in genres, students can add to their own imaginative resources and come to an awareness not only of how to write, but of what to write. In this way, writing instruction can both encourage students to express their ideas in individually authentic voices and to make texts that are socially appropriate.

Demonstration

In Section One of this book we considered some of the reasons why it might be important to teach writing skills. We also discussed some of the different approaches that teachers and textbook authors have adopted. In Section Two, we will look at various practical solutions that have been proposed for the teaching of writing.

In 7 we will review, with reference to Section One, what students need to learn in order to be able to write successfully in general language learning settings. In the rest of this section we will consider materials that have been specifically prepared to teach writing. We will look at the way in which context and content create a framework for writing (8 and 9), then consider the teaching of specific writing skills (10), and finally review these different approaches by discussing ways of giving feedback on student writing (11).

7 Writing in language teaching

7.1 Identifying purpose

'Writing' is included as an element in most language teaching course-books, but it is sometimes difficult to decide what the purpose of the writing activities is.

▶ **TASK 40**

Two writing tasks are given on pages 66 and 67. Example 1 is taken from a writing skills book, from a unit on writing telegrams. Example 2 comes at the end of unit in a general English course-book dealing with dreams, psychology, psychoanalysis, and the supernatural. As you review these tasks, ask yourself why the students are being asked to carry them out.

There is, clearly, a difference between the objectives of the activities. Example 1 aims to provide the learner with an awareness of the differences in language use that are associated with different written media. It has the specific purpose of developing the learner as a *writer*, and the outcomes of the task can be described accordingly. In such a context success can be measured by comparing one student's work with another and seeing whose text communicates most effectively—at the lowest possible cost in pence per word! If students who initially had difficulty doing this sort of task learn how to do it successfully, then it could be said that a new writing skill had been acquired.

Example 2, taken from a general language teaching coursebook, is more limited in its scope but is also more demanding. In it the authors are basically saying 'Now it's your turn'. A series of stories has been told in the earlier part of the unit and the writing task has been included both to allow for the expression of the learner's own experience, and also to prepare students for language examinations. The writing is given primarily as a homework task and no particular purpose or audience is specified. For the student responding to the task in Example 2 there can be no objective measure of success. Task fulfilment will depend on the student's life experience—or willingness to be inventive—and his or her knowledge of similar texts. No additional input is given to help the student form an appropriate text, and no criteria for evaluation are implied in the task specification. The possibilities for failure or dissatisfaction are very high, though given the right student and the right context, the

Example 1

Task 2

Sonia wants to contact her mother quickly. Her mother has no telephone, so Sonia sent her an Intelpost message.

Now write the telegram Sonia might have written instead of the Intelpost message. Remember, the cost of sending a telegram is 25p per word, including the address. Sonia doesn't want to spend more than £10 on the telegram.

Intelpost

For Post Office use only			
A Royal Mail Special Service	Transaction number	Time	Year Month Day

Transmitting office stamp

Receiving office stamp

To be completed by the sender

Sender's name
Sonia Whitting

Address
℅ WALTER SCOTT INN
Inverness.

Postcode

Phone number
Inverness 3478

Please write your message in the space below in black ink

To be delivered to (name)
MRS JAMES

Address
30, DANE STREET
SOUTHAMPTON

Postcode
SO9 4YQ

Phone number

Service requirement
(see notes overleaf for details)
1 ☒ Same day delivery
2 ☐ Next day delivery

3 ☐ Greetings card number

Dear Mum,

Don't get worried when you read this letter. I'm sending it by special delivery because we need money quickly. We've had a small accident, nothing very serious fortunately, but Jeremy's broken his arm and the car is just a wreck. Still, we were lucky that it wasn't worse ... Right now, we're staying in Inverness, at the Walter Scott Inn (tel. Inverness 3478) We have to stay here a few days : Jeremy will leave the hospital tonight, but we'd better all rest a few days before travelling back. And we have to do something about the car. Could you please send us £300 here as quickly as you can?

I phoned the insurance, but could you give them a ring and make sure everything is all right. (All the details are in the drawer of my desk.) And if you could ring Jane and cancel our Tuesday appointment?

I'm sorry to send you such a letter but you really mustn't worry. We are all fine now and looking forward to seeing you very soon. Ring us here if you can.

Lots of love,

Sonia.

(*Boutin et al.* 1987:34)

Example 2

Either write a short account of a dream you remember
vividly *or* write a short account of a supernatural event that
happened to you or a friend.

(*Abbs and Freebairn 1982:92*)

task provides a stimulating language development activity. Success in
such an activity could be said, however, to depend on the learner already
possessing a well-developed capacity to write in a literary manner. In
other words, the task does not provide a framework for teaching new
writing skills.

These two examples represent different sides of 'writing' in published
teaching materials: activities that are designed to develop the skills of
the apprentice writer (Example 1), and activities that assume the learner's
general competence as a writer and which provide the opportunity for
practising the target language (Example 2). As 'writing' can figure in
language learning materials in such different ways, it is sometimes difficult to establish the specific purpose of a particular writing activity. It
can also be difficult to say with any confidence what a 'good' writing
activity is.

7.2 What writers need to know

One way of addressing these problems is to consider what it is that
writers need to know in order to write effectively, and then to see to
what extent writing tasks in published materials make provision for this.

In Section One we considered a range of approaches to the teaching of
writing, and concluded that there was considerable scope for an
approach which both emphasized knowledge about the context and content of a piece of writing—a focus on genre, and also took into account
how a piece of writing was carried out—a focus on process. In such a
view, the successful writer has to have content knowledge, context
knowledge, language system knowledge, and writing process knowledge
(see 5.5).

content knowledge
Knowledge of the concepts involved in the subject area

context knowledge
Knowledge of the social context in which the text will be read, including the reader's expectations, and knowledge of the co-texts alongside
which this new text will be read

language system knowledge
Knowledge of those aspects of the language system (e.g. lexis, syntax)
that are necessary for the completion of the task

writing process knowledge
Knowledge of the most appropriate way of preparing for a writing task.

In other words it was argued that if writers know what to write in a given context, what the reader expects the text to look like in a given context, and which parts of the language system are relevant to the particular task in hand, and has a command of writing skills appropriate to this task, then they have a good chance of writing something that will be effective.

The way in which these sets of knowledge interrelate is shown in the diagram below:

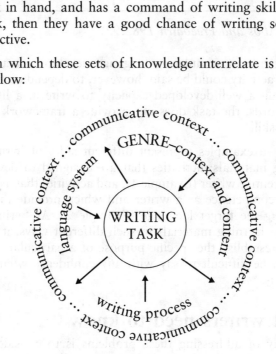

Figure 4

This represents the way in which, for any writing task, a successful writer draws on knowledge of the genre (content and context), knowledge of the language system, and knowledge of appropriate writing processes.

Thus a report-writing task can give students an opportunity to:

- understand the content area that the report deals with
- investigate the probable relationship between reader and writer in the context in question
- find out about aspects of the language system that are useful when writing this sort of text
- extend or practise appropriate writing skills.

A writing task of this kind is likely to actively engage students as apprentice writers, in other words to help them in the process of *learning to write*.

If, on the other hand, a task provides little or no means for students to extend their knowledge of appropriate content, to investigate and learn about the context, to enhance their understanding of the language system, or to become more skilled as writers, even though they have to write in order to complete the task, it is more likely to be one that is using *writing to learn* the language. Although this distinction between learning to write and writing to learn is in no sense black and white, it does provide a basis for thinking about writing tasks in language teaching materials.

▶ TASK 41

Given below and overleaf are four activities from contemporary general language teaching materials, all of which involve writing. Using the framework that we have just discussed, how effective do you feel these tasks are likely to be in helping learners to develop their competence as writers (i.e. learning to write)?

Example 1

C Plan a page of a brochure intended for one of these two audiences:

either   fairly well-off tourists or businesspeople on expenses
or   penniless students or hard-up travellers

In groups produce a page of a colour brochure (similar to the first page of this unit) about a town or city other than London. Suggest three or four places (illegible text) for the audience you have chosen. Plan the page design carefully so that it will look attractive to your readers.

Decide exactly what pictures you would want, then write a description of each one so that an artist could draw it, or so that a picture researcher could find a photograph as close as possible to what you want.

(*Willis and Willis 1988:82*)

Example 2

Listening and note taking

| T.28 | Listen to the talk and make notes under the headings above.
When you have finished compare your notes with another student's.

(*Soars and Soars 1987:86*)

Example 3

2 Look at the picture for two minutes. Then close your book. Work with a partner, and make as many sentences as you can with *some*. Examples:

There are some books on the tables.

There's some ice outside the window.

(*Swan and Walter 1990:34*)

Example 4

> 3 | T.26 | Listen to the
> conversation on tape.
> The Prime Minister is being
> interviewed about a proposed pay
> increase for politicians of thirty-
> five per cent.
> Report the conversation.
> The following verbs might help.
>
> explain   insist   refuse
>
> > point out
> >
> > go on to say   that. . .
> >
> > deny
>
> > tell someone that. . .
>
> Begin like this.
> The Prime Minister began by saying
> that he had the situation under
> control, and that there was no crisis.
> He was asked. . .

(*Soars and Soars 1987:81*)

Example 1. The writing task in this activity is not the production of the brochure itself, but rather the preparation of an 'art brief' for an artist or picture researcher to work from. If the task were worked through quickly, with the teacher as the only reader of the texts, then it is possible that there would be little development of an awareness of content and context, language system, or writing processes. However, the task has considerable potential for helping learners *learn to write* if the teacher creates a context for writing by dividing the class into 'art-brief writers' and 'artists or picture researchers' and, if possible, supplies a stock of pictures cut from magazines for the 'picture researchers' to select from, and art materials that the 'artists' can use. In this kind of context the 'art-brief writers' can work in small groups while preparing their descriptions, together developing their awareness of the writing processes involved in selecting clear, unambiguous language and organizing it in the most reader-friendly way.

If the teacher gives the learners an opportunity to work in more than one role, i.e. both as 'art-brief writers' and 'artists or picture researchers' they will also have the experience of working with the descriptions that have been prepared by other groups, thereby gaining a better idea of how, in order to produce a useful piece of writing, a writer has to be able to understand the needs of the likely reader. So far as genre knowledge is concerned, this kind of activity will provide learners with the opportunity to develop a control of the sorts of genre that Martin discusses in his comments on the difference between reports and descriptions (see **6.2**).

Example 2 clearly requires students to write, but to what end? As a note-making activity it draws on skills that they may have already developed—so in this instance it does not attempt to teach a writing skill. However, as the task also requires learners to compare notes with one another it helps them to enhance their ability to identify salient information in a listening text and to record the information in a way that can be easily understood at a later point. While note-making is not the same as composing and might, therefore, traditionally not be considered a skill that needs to be taught by a teacher of writing, it is perhaps one of the things that is most often done *with* writing, and can be an essential pre-writing skill. In this sense it can be thought of as a skill related to writing and there is, therefore, an argument for considering note-making activities as tasks that help learners in *learning to write*. This is especially the case when follow-up activities, as in Example 2, encourage learners to compare their own notes with those of other students, and, ideally, where these notes are then used in subsequent writing tasks which extend their understanding of genre and the language system.

Example 3, by contrast, seems to be using writing to support language learning objectives other than the development of writing skills—it is basically a grammar practice exercise. Although such exercises necessarily involve writing things down (and it is perhaps the case that the generation of correct graphological sentences is a useful preparation for writing), the primary focus of this activity is the revision of the expression *some*. While the activity encourages co-operative learning and text production, writing is an incidental part of the task. A need to write has been created by the task designers: the learners need a common means for recording their joint perceptions of the picture. To ask the learners to write single decontextualized sentences with a common grammatical form may be justified in language learning terms. However, as it does nothing to assist learners in developing their appreciation of writing skills, genre, or the relationship between communicative purpose and the language system, this type of activity is best seen as a *writing to learn* exercise.

Example 4 is of a similar type to Example 3. The coursebook writers' purpose here seems to be to provide a review activity which will help consolidate an area of grammar (reported speech) that has been presented in an earlier task, so in this sense Example 4 is also a *writing to learn* exercise.

7.3 Conclusion

We have now seen that not all language learning activities which make use of writing will help a learner to write more effectively—many simply depend on a previously established capacity to write in order to practise other aspects of the language. We have also seen that it is possible to consider the ways in which learners can be helped to write more effectively in terms of four different sets of knowledge: content knowledge and context knowledge (genre); knowledge of the language system, and knowledge of appropriate writing processes. In the sections which follow we shall look at teaching materials from these different perspectives.

8   Writing in business and professional settings

8.1   Writing in different contexts

In **7** we noted that successful writers need to be clear about four inter-dependent sets of knowledge when undertaking a writing task: (1) knowledge of the content that is required by the writing task; (2) knowledge of the context in which the text is being written; (3) knowledge of those aspects of the language system that are relevant to the writing task, and (4) knowledge of appropriate writing processes, for example planning and reviewing. We also saw that the different communicative purposes of writing activities will determine to a large extent the way in which apprentice writers will use this knowledge.

 TASK 42

In **1.1** we considered why three students might need to learn how to write in a foreign or second language. Consider two of these students once more and think about the immediate contexts in which they need to write:

– Why do they need to write?
– Who will they write for?
– What will they write about?

1 *Larissa Skopinskaya*. Larissa is nineteen and works in the Personnel Department of a St Petersburg bank. She is studying for an internationally recognized English language examination in order to get herself a new job with a multinational organization.

2 *Charles Nolotshungo*. Charles, who is thirty-two, lives in South Africa and works in the Public Health Department of Cape Town City Council. His education has been interrupted because of social disruption so he is studying English as part of an evening course in accountancy. He also wants to set up his own firm.

Charles' immediate need is to write in a narrow range of genres for his accountancy examinations, although he will also soon need to know how to write a good business plan so that he can get financial support for his new company. He has very different immediate objectives from

Larissa, who is studying in order to meet the requirements of the Cambridge First Certificate. Each student needs to write for a different kind of readership, and needs to produce different kinds of text. Although it is important for them to develop a *general* ability to plan and compose written texts, such general training on its own would not prepare them to face the contrasting demands and constraints involved in using English in their chosen fields. In 8 and 9 we will look at the ways in which teaching materials can help learners address differing needs. We will consider these materials from the points of view of these two sorts of learner:

– students who want to become more effective writers in business or professional settings
– students who need to become more effective writers in order to be able to study another subject, or to take language examinations in a foreign language.

This will only be a partial account of the range of contexts for which student writers may wish to prepare. It will, however, give an indication of some of the ways in which teaching materials can help learners gain the kinds of knowledge that they need if they are to become competent writers.

8.2 Business and professional contexts

There are two main categories of student who wish to develop foreign language writing skills for business and professional settings: students preparing to enter the business world (pre-experience), and people already working in business (job-experienced). The consensus in materials designed for such learners is that both groups have largely similar learning needs. Taking English as an example, we find that both sets of students are assumed to need information on business practice in the international English-speaking business community, along with opportunities to develop their command of the language in a motivating context. Working from this premise, authors of Business English materials tend to use the behaviour, concepts, activities, and concerns of the international business world as a context for the development of language skills, and this includes writing skills. As these authors recognize the importance of cultural factors in professional communication—whether this is spoken or written—and the need of the learner to become aware of the ways in which speaking and writing styles can have a major impact on business success, their approach has many points of contact with the genre approach discussed in 6.

Given this emphasis on the context of business and professional communication, it is common for teaching materials which deal with business writing to present a range of language skills related to areas of professional activity such as those indicated in the following contents pages from some current materials from a Business English course.

Contents

(Jones and Alexander 1996:3)

One of the main approaches adopted in this type of material is to establish a context and then consider the language skills and knowledge that are relevant to it.

 ## TASK 43

In the example given below, which of the three business activities mentioned are likely to provide suitable contexts for the development of writing skills?

SITUATION

We are still at the offices of Bookmart Publishing Services. In this unit we see how to deal with problems of credit control; how to conduct an employee assessment interview; and how to investigate and report an accident.

CHARACTERS

George Harvey

Terry Cabe

Frank Penny

Mr Harris   owns a bookshop in York.

Mr Martinu   is General Manager at Martinu Books.

Andy Brumshaw   is the warehouse foreman at Bookmart.

Alice Perkins   is an office cleaner at Bookmart.

All these characters are British.

(*Owen 1992:57*)

Of the three activities, Owen exploits two as contexts for the development of writing skills—credit control and how to report an accident.

 ## TASK 44

In the section on credit control, the 'Document Study' activity gives the example below. As you study this extract, consider two questions:
- What do you think learners will understand by the instruction: 'Notice that it is very formal'?
- How useful do you feel this activity will be in helping learners to develop an appropriate style for their own business writing?

7.6 Document study: a formal letter

George Harvey has to write a letter to another bookshop, Martinu Books. They have not paid anything since the end of March. Read through the letter. Notice that it is very formal.

b^M BOOKMART
PUBLISHING
SERVICES LTD

Mr G F Martinu
General Manager
Martinu Books
Eastgate
York YO1 1DX

13 June 1991

Dear Mr Martinu

Our statements dated 31 March, 30 April and 31 May 1991

As we have received no reply to our letters of 4 May and 30 May, *we are compelled* to draw your attention once more to your non-payment of the sums owed to us. The total amount outstanding is now £15,872.87.

We regret that we cannot continue to allow credit terms as long as this debt remains uncleared. Until further notice, therefore, goods will be supplied to you only on receipt of cash against a pro forma invoice.

I shall be obliged if you will contact me personally within the next seven days to discuss means by which the amount outstanding can be cleared. We are anxious to avoid any action which might *jeopardise* the good business relationship *we have enjoyed* in the past.

Yours sincerely

G. H. Harvey

G A Harvey
Sales Manager

> **7.6**
> *we are compelled* we must; this is a very formal letter. *jeopardise* damage or destroy. *we have enjoyed* we have had; enjoy here does not suggest fun, it is another slightly formal expression.

(*Owen: 1992:59*)

One of the positive aspects of this activity is that learners are not asked to write immediately, but are encouraged to use the text as a source of linguistic and cultural information, and also as a potential model for future use. Students are also given some specific support to help them understand why the letter has been written in this particular way by means of the 'comment box' printed at the side of the page. This gives some basic information on the role and structure of formal letters in such contexts and could be expanded to give learners a more explicit appreciation of this aspect of written communication.

Both native and non-native speaker models can be useful to learners, but only if they are used in association with a critical framework which informs students what genre a particular text is a model of, and what features are distinctive of that genre. It is only then that a text can provide information which will be helpful to students who wish to develop their own writing style for a particular context. With this in mind, it would be possible to extend the task provided in the extract from Owen. As we saw in **6**, the kinds of activity that can be helpful here are those which enable learners to understand how social context influences the way in which writers make textual, grammatical, and lexical choices. By close study of model texts, students will find ways of investigating language use which they can draw on when doing their own writing. A simple example of such a technique is given below. This activity enables students to investigate the ways in which language use in business correspondence is involved in establishing formal relationships, and would make a helpful supplement to the activity in Task 44. In this particular instance, two words that have high frequency in a particular type of formal business correspondence have been selected—'unfortunately' and 'pleased'.

▶ **TASK 45**

The texts in the concordance below were written by several different writers in the same office in a non-governmental organization. Consider the following questions regarding the use of 'pleased' and 'unfortunately' in two distinct genres of writing in administrative contexts.

```
 1    idered your application and I am   pleased to inform you that Xxxxxx Xxxxx
 2    sting and valuable one, and I am   pleased to learn of the contribution from t
 3      t the Edinburgh Festival. I am   pleased to be able to offer you a contribut
 4      Dear Professor Xxxxxxxxxx, I am   pleased to be able to assist with the fundi
 5    Festival on behalf of XXXX. I am   pleased to tell you that we will be able to
 6    my of Art later this month. I am   pleased to tell you that we will be able to
 7      their performance in Oslo. I am   pleased to tell you that the Xxxxxx Xxxxxxx
 8      our scholarship programme. I am   pleased to be able to tell you that you hav
 9      our scholarship programme. I am   pleased to be able to tell you that you hav
10       Sakala Street, Tallinn. I am   pleased to know that you are already in tou
11       of your time in the UK. I am   pleased to be able to tell you that the Dir
12    to the interview last week. I am   pleased to tell you that we have sent your
13    is award earlier this year. I am   pleased to be able to tell you that you hav
14    ch a successful partnership, and   pleased to be able to tell you that the Xxx
15      ing her visit. We would also be   pleased to host a meeting for her to talk a
16       Professor Xxxxxx, You will be   pleased to know that we have been able to p
17      uage Unit - Latvia You will be   pleased to hear that we have now prepared a
18    member of your Office I would be   pleased to attend such a meeting along with
19    l it would be useful, I would be   pleased to talk to you in a more detail on my
20      are in Tallinn we would be very   pleased if you could run a couple of sessio
21      can hope to satisfy, and we are   unfortunately unable to offer you any finan
22    fore writing to say that we are,   unfortunately, unable to offer you any assi
23    fore writing to say that we are,   unfortunately, unable to offer you any assi
24    rtment in London about this but,   unfortunately, they are unable to help this
25    o Xxxxxx. the Xxxxxx Xxxxxxxx is   unfortunately, unable to help you with the fundi
26    nd offer of support. We are not,   unfortunately, in a position to establish a
27    n interesting one, but we do not   unfortunately have sufficient budget availa
28    5, and I am writing to say that,   unfortunately, we will not be able to offer
29    d I am writing to tell you that,   unfortunately, we have not been able to of
30    If of Xxxxxx Veterinary Academy.   Unfortunately, we are unable to help you wi
31    ve you an application form. c.   Unfortunately, we are unable to help you wi
32    id, to follow up our phone call.   Unfortunately, the Xxxxxx Xxxxxxxx will not
33    g Sustainable Rural Development.   Unfortunately, the timing of this course ma
34    isit the University of Xxxxxxxxxx.   Unfortunately we have far more demands on o
35    onomies of Transition in Xxxxxx.   Unfortunately, as you will realise, we have
36       hraseology to be held in Leeds.   Unfortunately we are not able to contribute
37    r any assistance in this matter.   Unfortunately I am also unable to suggest t
```

> – In which genres have the texts used in these examples been written?
> – What degree of personal responsibility do the writers take for the implications of what they are writing? Does this differ according to the genres you have identified?
> – What evidence does the concordance data provide regarding the likely antonyms of 'unfortunately' and 'pleased' in these contexts? Will they be 'fortunately' and 'displeased'?

Even with the tiny amount of data given here, it is not difficult to conclude that the majority of these extracts come from texts related to the genres of 'Offer letters' and 'Rejection letters'. The data also reveals how writers have tended to distance themselves from unpleasant news by, for example, using *we* as the grammatical subject of 'bad news' statements, but have put themselves in the foreground in the cases where good news is being given, for example using phrases like: *I am pleased to* . . . .

With this sort of data, students can begin to investigate the ways in which polite distance is systematically established in written English, and the implications of different degrees of distance for the reader–writer relationship. In this way, texts are no longer just models, they become resources that students can use to develop a broader competence as writers.

As we noted in **6.7**, this sort of analysis does not necessarily require access to computers. And such an approach has the potential both to provide useful models and to help students come to a better understanding of how communicative purpose determines the way in which language is used in different contexts. It offers a richer resource than the study of a single (often inauthentic) text. Learners and teachers can investigate a variety of examples in order to answer questions such as: 'Why is this text written this way?' and 'How can this text help me achieve my own objectives as a writer?'

▶ TASK 46

How does the following example from Business English teaching material provide an opportunity for learners to move beyond imitation?

UNIT 2

Achieving a Tone to Suit the Business Reader

Good writers in the business world know how to choose their words. The communication must achieve its goal or time and energy are wasted. If you wish to be a good writer, good grammar and spelling are necessary but not sufficient. Your words must be chosen with care and tested for their suitability for each particular writing task. Good writers can write **upwards** and **downwards** without offending their readers. They use the most suitable expressions for their position and particular business.

The notion of tone is very important to the business writer. Since readers can be insulted not by the message but by the manner of expression, an otherwise perfect memo or letter could quite possibly cause a breakdown in communication. It is therefore important for you to be able to analyse your relationship with your reader(s) and then to choose the appropriate language and tone for your message.

```
TO:      Y

FROM:    X

SUBJECT: Damage to Company Furniture


It has been brought to my attention that an increasing
amount of damage to company furniture has occurred in recent
weeks.

This damage has generally taken place while furniture was
being moved into or out of rented accommodation. It seems
that, on each occasion, the labourers may have been working
without supervision. It is possible that such damage could
be avoided if stricter levels of supervision were
maintained.

Therefore, it is felt that a responsible member of the
General Services Department should be present whenever
labourers are moving company furniture. The presence of this
person might ensure the reduction of unnecessary damage and
subsequent expense to the company.

If accepted, this proposal ought to come into immediate
effect. Your comments would be greatly appreciated.
```

Evaluation Exercise 1

Look at these two memoranda. Read them with the aim of appreciating the differences and similarities. The second memo is from Y to Z.

▶ 5

```
SUBJECT: Damage to Company Furniture


An unwarranted increase in the amount of damage to company
furniture has recently been noted.

This damage has taken place while furniture was being moved
into or out of rented accommodation. On each occasion, the
labourers were working without supervision. Such damage will
be avoided if strict levels of supervision are maintained.

Therefore, a responsible member of the General Services
Department must be present whenever labourers are moving
company furniture. The presence of this person will ensure
the reduction of unnecessary damage and subsequent expense
to the company.

Please nominate the individual to assume this responsibility
by 30 June 1985.

Thank you for your cooperation.
```

▶ 6

Discussion 1

You can see quite quickly that both memos cover exactly the same topic and contain the same information. The difference between them is in their tone. Writer X and Writer Y have used entirely different language. Look at the following simple organization chart. If we know that Writer X is the Senior Personnel Officer (Accommodation), we can quickly identify Writer Y.

```
         General Services Supt.
         |
         |                    Senior
 Accommodation            Personnel Officer
 Controller               ( Accommodation )
```

Writer Y is the General Services Superintendent and Z is the Accommodation Controller; this becomes clear when we analyse and compare the language used in the two memos. The Senior Personnel Officer uses quite a tentative and respectful tone when he writes his memo (Text 5) to his superior. On the other hand, the General Services Supt. shows his authority by writing his memo (Text 6) in a direct and decisive way.

The following table shows the major differences between the two texts.

Text 5 (Tentative)	Text 6 (Decisive)
—	(11) ... unwarranted ...
(14) ... generally ...	—
(15) It seems that ...	—
(16) ... may have been working ...	(15) ... were working ...
(17) It is possible that ...	—
(17) ... could be avoided ...	(15) ... will be avoided ...
(18) ... stricter ...	(16) ... strict ...
(18) ... were maintained ...	(16) ... are maintained ...
(110) ... it is felt that ...	—
(111) ... should be present ...	(18) ... must be present ...
(113) ... might ensure ...	(19) ... will ensure ...

Note in particular how a single word can set the tone of a piece of writing; this is demonstrated very clearly in Text 6 by the word *unwarranted*. Notice also that a letter, memo, etc., with a tentative tone tends to be rather longer; this is mainly caused by the use of such expressions as *It seems that . . .*, *It is possible that . . .*, etc.

(Doherty, Knapp, and Swift 1987:13–15)

Although the other materials we have considered have also presented *contrasting* examples, the differences between those examples have not been fully accounted for. In the example in Task 46, however, there is an explicit discussion of the power relations that can exist between readers and writers in business settings, and an account of the way in which language use changes in different power relationships. Although the discussion does not give a complete account of the topic, it provides an explanation which is sufficient for learners to draw on in future writing tasks, and which enables them to understand how choices from the grammatical and lexical systems of the language have an impact on the way in which writers and readers interact.

8.3 Conclusion

In our brief survey of published Business English teaching materials we have seen that they can provide appropriate text examples for students to work with. Some also allow for an investigation of *why* texts have been worded in particular ways for specific contexts. However published materials can be supplemented by the provision of a much broader range of examples for investigation, and the development of analytical and critical methodologies such as concordancing in order to build an explicit account of language use in specific contexts. By these means, learners can be helped to come to a better understanding of the interaction between context, content, and communicative purpose.

9 Writing in academic and study settings

9.1 Introduction

We saw in 8 that learners who wish to develop writing skills for business communication face the double task of gaining an awareness of a new business culture *and* a new language skill. For job-experienced learners, their motivation may well be that they are operating in a context where feedback has 'real life' significance and is not just provided by a teacher. They know that when they write a business letter or prepare a report, if the expectations of their readers are disappointed, or if those readers feel confused or patronized, they themselves as business writers risk losing business!

Similarly, learners who wish to write in new academic settings have to gain a mastery of the concepts and content of their subject area as well as developing an ability to express themselves effectively and appropriately in the foreign language. Even if they are established scholars, writing in a foreign language remains a challenging and complex task; they cannot assume that the way things are done in the language of one culture will correspond exactly with the way things are done by expert writers in another.

In 7 we discussed the types of knowledge that a competent writer needs: content knowledge, context knowledge, writing process knowledge, and language system knowledge.

▶ TASK 47

If we set aside for the moment knowledge of the writing process (we shall discuss this in 10), in which of the remaining areas of knowledge do you feel that language teachers can be most helpful to learners who want to write for study purposes?

In most cases, language teachers can only be of limited help to their students in the area of content knowledge. Many language teachers in higher education find themselves having to teach aspects of the content of a specialist subject at the same time as teaching foreign language skills. This is often an unsatisfactory experience, as their own knowledge of the subject is usually limited. One way round the problem is close co-operation between language teachers and subject specialists in the development of writing programmes.

Context knowledge and language system knowledge are, on the other hand, areas where language teachers do have relevant expertise. We will be focusing on these in the rest of 9 and considering ways in which published teaching materials can help learners to gain a fuller understanding of writing in an academic context.

9.2 The intellectual/rhetorical approach

▶ TASK 48

In your own experience of learning how to write for academic purposes, in either your first or second language, what would you say were your own teachers' starting points? Did they begin a course by working with complete texts, or with exercises to help you use different types of rhetorical device? Did they talk about the different writing skills that are required to write specific kinds of text such as essays or reports?

Broadly speaking, there are two contrasting views of what makes up the context of academic writing and how this context and the language use it generates can best be described. A long-standing tradition for teaching academic writing to first and second language learners in the English-speaking world, and in many European countries, assumes a common intellectual framework for *all* academic discourse—in other words a common academic context. In this tradition the modes of classical rhetoric, for example 'exposition' and 'description' are taken as the starting point for instruction in academic writing skills, and it is assumed that students have a primary need to gain a mastery of these rhetorical modes if they are to become competent writers in their chosen disciplines. The list below provides an example of the content that is commonly taught in writing courses of this kind.

- Exposition
  Examples   Comparison and contrast
  Process   Definition
  Cause and effect   Division and classification

- Description
- Narration
- Argumentation and persuasion

(*Langan 1993:113*)

In teaching materials that are built around these categories, it is common for these rhetorical modes to be chapter headings. Examples of language use, and writing exercises, are provided to help students to express them in appropriate language. Once learners can control the exponents at sentence level, they move on to paragraph-length and then full text-length exercises. This is an approach to relating language system knowledge to context knowledge which we can call *intellectual / rhetorical.*

9.3 The social/genre approach

A contrasting approach takes as its starting point the concept of the *discourse community* and identifies not just one but a range of possible academic contexts. Swales describes six characteristics for identifying a group of writers and readers as a discourse community: there must be 'common goals, participatory mechanisms, information exchange, community specific genres, a highly specialized terminology and a high general level of expertise' (Swales 1990:29). Here, 'common goals' refers to the objectives of the scholars in any community: these can include accounts of replicable experimental procedures, the reporting of new knowledge, the examination of students, and so forth. In the case of writing, the 'participatory mechanisms' are the texts that are associated with a particular discipline. Examples include academic journals, textbooks, and the examinations that students have to write in order to proceed through their courses.

Teachers who work with this social view of the context of academic writing will ask their students to discover how their own specific discourse communities function and how this affects the way in which members of that community write. In this process of discovery learners will look closely at the relationships that exist between different readers and writers and, in doing so, their primary data will be the texts themselves. These can be analysed, imitated, and, as the learner becomes more proficient, may well be challenged and transformed. We should note that such an investigative approach will often include a consideration of modes of rhetoric, not as models for imitation, but as examples of ways of writing that students should be aware of. They will form a part of the study, therefore, but will not be the prime organizational feature for teaching materials. We can call this approach to writing *social / genre.*

Three important aspects of this approach to academic writing exploit context and language system knowledge These are:

– structure and organization
– argumentation
– style

The two approaches to teaching academic writing we have mentioned— *intellectual / rhetorical and social / genre* – deal with these aspects in different ways.

9.4 Structure and organization

▶ TASK 49

Extract A below comes from a widely used writing course for students with academic or professional needs. Extract B comes from a course on writing laboratory reports. What differences can you identify in the way that the authors present information about the structure and organization of written texts?

Extract A

Task 4

The lines of this traditional nursery rhyme have been disorganized; try to rewrite it with the lines in their correct order. If there are generally recognizable structures for texts, it should be possible to agree to a sensible version of this text. Work with a partner, and check your recomposition with another pair or students afterwards.

> The Queen of Hearts
> And took them clean away
> He stole the tarts
>
> The Knave* of Hearts
> and beat the Knave full sore
> Called for the tarts
>
> The Knave of Hearts
> All on a summer's day
> She made some tarts
>
> The King of Hearts
> And vowed he'd steal no more
> Brought back the tarts.

*knave = a picture card in a deck of cards; (in old English) a dishonest man.

The reason it is possible to agree on a sensible version of the above rhyme is that it has a predictable text structure:

situation → problem → solution → evaluation

situation answers the question:
    'What are we talking about?'   In this text, the Queen's cakes.

problem answers the question:
    a) 'Why are we talking about this?'   Because there is a problem.
    b) 'What is the problem?'   In this text, the Knave stole the tarts.

solution answers the question:
    'What is to be/has been done?'   In this text the King calls for the
                                                              tarts and beats the Knave.

evaluation answers the question:
    'How good is the solution?'   In this text apparently very good
                                                              because the Knave promises never to
                                                              steal again.

(*Hamp-Lyons and Heasley 1987:100*)

Extract B

---

1 Model Report

Before we look at different ways of writing up a report, we will look at a model report and the language used in it.

The report is about an experiment to find the resistivity of iron. The resistivity is a constant which is a measure of the electric resisting power of a substance. It is defined as the resistance offered by a one metre cube of the material. The resistivity is represented by the symbol p and is given by the formula

$p = \dfrac{RA}{l}$ where R is the resistance of a uniform conductor of length l and cross-sectional area A.

Read through the report and look for answers to the questions which follow it.

[Full text of laboratory report follows.]

Questions

1. What are the headings in the report?
2. What are the aims of the different sections of the report? Choose the best alternative in the following:
   (a) The introduction is concerned with:
      (i) the theory of the experiment
      (ii) the method for carrying out the experiment; or
      (iii) the theory of the experiment and the method for carrying it out.

(*Dudley-Evans 1985:5–8*)

These extracts represent two strongly differentiated lines of thought on the teaching of academic discourse. The first takes the view that students need a strong grasp of the most highly generalizable accounts of text organization. It then becomes their responsibility to implement this understanding in their own subject areas. Such an approach, essentially an intellectual / rhetorical one, has many advantages, chief among which is that it has the potential to be used with students of writing from a wide range of learning situations. The theory is that if students complete the course, they will be able to cope with a broad range of real-world writing problems as and when they arise. The coursebook can be used with different kinds of student; he or she develops the ability to deal with new textual problems as and when they arise. Thus Hamp-Lyons and Heasley's book does not attempt to give specific information about how, say, historians, language students, or earth scientists organize their texts. Rather, the authors draw the learner's attention to the common rhetorical patterns that can be found in many texts: GENERAL – PARTICULAR; SITUATION–PROBLEM–SOLUTION/RESPONSE-EVALUATION/RESULT, and so forth. While this should have the benefit that learners will develop an understanding of how texts work, there can be problems. One of the most important is that students may feel that the examples of texts presented in the materials, along with the activities that they are asked to carry out, are so distant from their immediate needs or interests that they are unwilling to suspend disbelief for the purpose of the task in hand.

The second extract reflects a social / genre approach. It provides learners with highly specific information about the forms of text required by the genre of 'Report of laboratory experiment'. This way of working has different advantages and disadvantages. Learner motivation can be high as students with relevant interests can see an immediate return on their investment. Also, the function of grammatical and lexical features in the development of a text can be demonstrated more clearly, thereby making explicit the relationship between language form, meaning, and communicative purpose. This link can be further clarified by organizing the instructional materials around chapter headings such as: 'Title and aim'; 'Procedure'; 'Results and discussion of results', and 'Comparison of results'. The main disadvantages of such an approach is that this kind of book will only appeal to a narrow range of learners. Moreover, because of its relatively narrow focus, it is difficult for learners to generalize from the insights gained in writing laboratory reports to writing other kinds of text.

This latter sort of instructional material can also be criticized, as we have seen in our discussion of process approaches in 6, as being overly prescriptive in imposing a model on learners and making little allowance for individual creativity. Such a challenge can be countered by two arguments: first, students are encouraged to analyse texts, and the skills they develop in dealing with texts typical of one genre can be transferred to other genres; second, learners in higher education courses have a well-documented capacity to pick and choose from the range of interpretations and models that might be on offer (see Swales 1990:29-31). There remains, however, the fact that some learners may feel imposed upon if they are faced with this sort of highly structured learning material. This underscores the responsibility that teachers have when selecting textbooks.

In the examples above, learners have been asked to infer an organization pattern by analysing examples of texts in which the pattern is implicit. In those that follow, the teaching materials make these patterns more explicit.

▶ TASK 50

The text outlines given below are typical of the three different categories of academic writing which learners need to be able to produce.
- Identify the categories
- In addition to these outlines, what sort of data would learners need to have in order to develop an understanding of text organization for each one?

Extract 1

Preliminaries	1	The title
	2	Acknowledgements
	3	List of contents
	4	List of figures / tables
Introduction	5	The abstract
	6	Statement of the problem
Main body	7	Review of the literature
	8	Design of the investigation
	9	Measurement techniques used
	10	Results
Conclusion	11	Discussion and conclusion
	12	Summary of conclusions
Extras	13	Bibliography
	14	Appendices

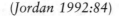

(*Jordan 1992:84*)

Extract 2

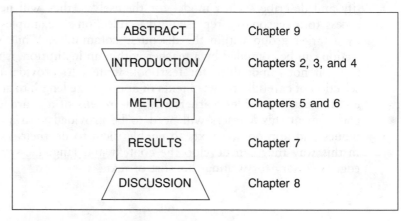

(*Weissberg and Buker 1990:3*)

Extract 3

Definition:	What is tourism?
Situation:	What is the present situation regarding tourism? How did it come about? What are the main features of tourism?
Problem:	Is there a problem? If so, what is it?
Solution/ Response:	How can the problem be dealt with? What alternative solutions are there? What constraints are there on each possible solution?
Evaluation:	Which of the solutions is likely to be the most effective? What would be the results of applying each of these solutions?

(*White and McGovern 1994:51*)

All three examples aim to make organizational features of texts clearer. They do this in different ways and make different demands on the student. All of them will require extensive knowledge on the part of the learner to make them operational. Extract 1 is an organizational framework derived from an extended piece of writing such as a dissertation, research report, or essay. It assumes that the student has previous knowledge of the genre in question and will already be familiar with abstracts, literature reviews, and bibliographies. In other words, a good deal of previous learning and teaching is assumed.

Extract 2, by contrast, represents a typical structure for a less extensive writing task—a report on an experimental procedure. The representation of this pattern is very abstract, however, and if learners are to identify and describe such a model for themselves, they will need to have access to a reasonably representative collection of examples of writing by a target group within the discourse community. While such a collection can be compiled by a teacher within an institution, it is less practical—if not impossible—for textbook writers to provide an unedited selection of carefully targeted texts of appropriate length to suit all learners. Extract 2 provides learners with the *results* of a genre analysis. To complement this learners will need to be provided with analytic techniques and appropriate texts to enable them to do their own analysis. In this way they can develop the context and language-system knowledge necessary for writing this sort of text.

Extract 3 is the most general of the organizational patterns given here—one that could have been derived from an expository essay or another form of argumentative writing. It draws on the minimal discourse pattern introduced in **4.5**, SITUATION–PROBLEM–SOLUTION/RESPONSE–EVALUATION/RESULT, a pattern useful to a broad cross-section of learners, whether in higher education courses or preparing to take a foreign language examination. Learners do, however, first need to identify this pattern in a range of easily accessible problem-oriented types of writing (for example newspaper articles), and learn to use it is as a way of organizing smaller and then larger texts. They will also need opportunities to deal with more specifically focused texts if they are to gain full competence as writers in a particular discourse community.

By whatever means students arrive at an understanding of the way in which texts are organized in their discourse communities, there remains the problem of how they can develop a capacity to write with confidence in a specific genre. In all of the cases we have considered so far, we have noted that students still need to apply these more general descriptions of texts to more specific writing. This brings us to the more particular level of argumentation.

9.5 Argumentation

▶ TASK 51

The two extracts below deal with the same aspect of the development of an argument—comparison and contrast—and also exemplify contrasting approaches to writing instruction. Which approach does each exemplify?

Extract 1

TASK 1

A description based on comparison and contrast can be developed in two ways:

1. You can group the main ideas about Subject A in one paragraph or section and the main ideas about Subject B in the next paragraph or section, in a 'vertical' movement, as in the first of the following diagrams.

2. Alternatively, you can treat the corresponding ideas on Subject A and Subject B as a pair and compare or contrast them one after the other, in a 'horizontal' movement, as in the second diagram.

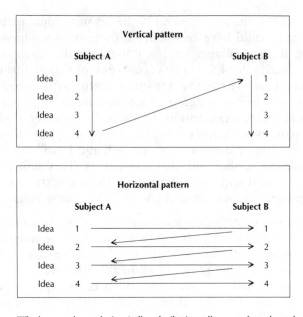

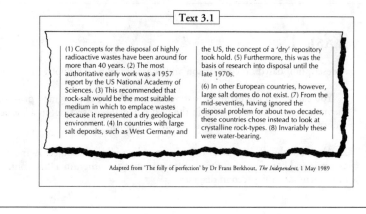

Whether you choose the 'vertical' or the 'horizontal' pattern depends on the kind of text you are writing, its purpose and your own preference. Some writers and readers find the 'horizontal' pattern clearer because it repeatedly reminds them of the comparison or contrast relationship. Others prefer the 'vertical' pattern because of its relative simplicity. The 'horizontal' pattern is often more suitable for a longer piece of writing. Both patterns are commonly used in descriptions involving comparison and contrast.

 Step 1

1.1 Read Text 3.1.

1.2 Consider the following questions:

    (a) Is the writer's description based on comparison or contrast – or both?
    (b) Has the writer used a 'vertical' or 'horizontal' pattern of organisation?
    (c) Which words are used to indicate a relationship of comparison or contrast? Can you think of similar words or phrases? (See Appendix 1.)

Text 3.1

(1) Concepts for the disposal of highly radioactive wastes have been around for more than 40 years. (2) The most authoritative early work was a 1957 report by the US National Academy of Sciences. (3) This recommended that rock-salt would be the most suitable medium in which to emplace wastes because it represented a dry geological environment. (4) In countries with large salt deposits, such as West Germany and the US, the concept of a 'dry' repository took hold. (5) Furthermore, this was the basis of research into disposal until the late 1970s.

(6) In other European countries, however, large salt domes do not exist. (7) From the mid-seventies, having ignored the disposal problem for about two decades, these countries chose instead to look at crystalline rock-types. (8) Invariably these were water-bearing.

Adapted from 'The folly of perfection' by Dr Frans Berkhout, *The Independent*, 1 May 1989

(*White and McGovern* 1994:22–4)

Extract 2

Stage 1   Comparison   1   Look at Tables 1 and 2.

Table 1: The Longest Rivers in the World

> 1 The Nile (Africa)—4,160 miles (6,695 kilometres)
> 2 The Amazon (South America)—4,080 miles (6,570 kilometres)
> 3 The Mississippi-Missouri (North America)—3,740 miles (6,020 kilometres)
> 4 The Yangtse (Asia: China)—3,430 miles (5,520 kilometres)

Table 2: Temperatures and Rainfall in Beijing, China

Month	J	F	M	A	M	J	J	A	S	O	N	D
Temperature (°C)	−4.7	−1.5	5.0	13.7	19.9	24.5	26.0	24.7	19.8	12.5	3.6	−2.6
Rainfall (cm)	0.2	0.5	0.5	1.5	3.6	7.6	23.9	16.0	6.6	1.5	0.8	0.2

top: the Nile (by satellite)
bottom: the Amazon (aerial view)

Note:
a the first month is January (J), the last is December (D).
b the temperature is measured in Centigrade, and is an average.
c the rainfall is measured in centimetres, and is also an average.

Now complete the following sentences. If necessary, look at *Appendix 7: Comparisons*. Put one or more words in each space.

Table 1:

1 The Nile is _____ the Mississippi–Missouri.
2 The Amazon is _____ long _____ the Nile.
3 The Nile is _____ river in the world.
4 The Mississippi–Missouri is _____ the Amazon.
5 The Yangtse is _____ river in China.

Table 2:

6 In Beijing, January is a _____ month _____ _____ December.
7 July is a _____ month _____ June.
8 There is _____ rain in May _____ in March.
9 July has the _____ rain; in other words, July is _____ month.
10 August is _____ warm _____ July.
11 December and January are _____ months.
12 The rainfall in February is _____ in March.
13 April is _____ wet _____ October.
14 The rainfall in November is _____ in May.
15 July is the _____ month, and also _____ month.

2   Look at Table 3.

Table 3: The Highest Mountains in the World

> 1 Everest (Nepal/Tibet)—29,028 feet (8,848 metres)
> 2 K2 (Kashmir/Sinkiang)—28,250 feet (8,611 metres)
> 3 Kangchenjunga (Nepal/Sikkim)—28,168 feet (8,586 metres)
> 4 Makalu (Nepal/Tibet)—27,805 feet (8,475 metres)
> 5 Dhaulagiri (Nepal)—26,810 feet (8,172 metres)

Note: All the mountains above are in the Himalayas.

(*Jordan* 1992:49–50)

The White and McGovern materials work in a top-down way, giving learners an overview of typical organizational patterns for this type of description and then providing them with an opportunity to work as analysts and editors before they work in the genre themselves. We can say that such an approach moves from 'text' to 'writing activity'. Throughout this process students discuss and share experiences. Reference materials which provide examples of language use associated with comparison and contrast are supplied in an appendix. An advantage of this activity is that, at this point in the unit of work, the learners do not need to be inventive. Instead, they are given practice in operating on written language that is appropriate to a particular category of text. In this sense the materials bring together ideas that we have seen in genre and process approaches to the teaching of writing, and therefore conform more closely to a social / genre view of writing.

The Jordan materials approach the problem from a different starting point and use a bottom-up approach. Here learners are given data to work on and then asked to complete exercises of sentence length with a progressively more and more open structure. The materials are typical of a rhetorical / intellectual approach to writing instruction. They use a 'Presentation, Practice, Production' cycle in order to help learners gain control of the skills they need in the target language. The movement here is from 'writing activity' to 'text'.

▶ **TASK 52**

> Look at the extracts in Task 51 again. Do you feel that there are any advantages or disadvantages to either approach?

It is possible that with learners who have limited control of sentence-level grammatical relationships there are advantages in using the bottom-up approach favoured by Jordan. Students (and teachers) are given a secure and systematic means of controlling a set of rhetorical modes, and learners can work with the materials independently because there are keys to most of the exercises. This way of working also makes it possible to plan classes in which a discrete set of information is dealt with in a controlled way. A disadvantage of this approach is that insufficient emphasis may be paid to complete texts and learners do not have the opportunity to develop their ability to edit and revise texts with a view to improving communicative quality. In other words, work at this level may not ultimately transfer to higher levels of text organization.

Such a transfer may be more readily achieved in the White and McGovern materials since they focus on discourse organization and help learners to match language use to communicative purpose. This does, of course, presuppose a relatively high degree of sophistication on the learner's part, but this is not an unreasonable presupposition in higher education settings. The remaining tasks in this chapter of their book are consistent with this philosophy, requiring discussion, investigation, and the discovery of rules or patterns. Although this way of working may be demanding of teachers and learners alike, it does require learners to do the things that they will eventually have to do as effective writers in 'real-life' contexts, and also provides them with strategies for self-editing, co-operative editing, and peer reviewing. In short, such an approach allows for integration between the level of argumentation and the higher level of text organization.

9.6 Style

Students need to know about the typical structure and organization of texts associated with the genres in which they have to write, and need to gain control over different modes of argumentation. They also need to be able to express themselves in the most effective and appropriate style for the context in which they are writing.

 TASK 53

The following text extracts were presented to 1,580 scientists and academics in an experiment which investigated writing style in academic settings. Respondents were asked to say which text they preferred, and to evaluate the quality of thinking of the two writers. Which do you prefer? Why?

Brown's version

In the first experiment of the series using mice it was discovered that total removal of the adrenal glands effects reduction of aggressiveness and that aggressiveness in adrenalectomized mice is restorable to the level of intact mice by treatment with corticosterone. These results point to the indispensability of the adrenals for the full expression of aggression. Nevertheless, since adrenalectomy is followed by an increase in the release of adrenocorticotrophic hormone (ACTH), and since ACTH has been reported (Brain, 1972) to decrease the aggressiveness of intact mice, it is possible that the effects of adrenalectomy on aggressiveness are a function of the concurrent increased levels of ACTH. [*107 words, continued for another 80*]

Smith's version

The first experiment in our series with mice showed that total removal of the adrenal glands reduces aggressiveness. Moreover, when treated with corticosterone, mice that had their adrenals taken out became as aggressive as intact animals again. These findings suggest that the adrenals are necessary for animals to show full aggressiveness.

But removal of the adrenals raises the levels of adrenocorticotrophic hormone (ACTH), and Brain found that ACTH lowers

the aggressiveness of intact mice. Thus the reduction of aggressiveness after this operation might be due to the higher levels of
ACTH which accompany it. [*96 words, continued for another 80*]

(*Turk and Kirkman 1989:17–18*)

Smith's version was the one preferred by the majority of respondents
(69.5 per cent)—and over 75 per cent reported that they considered
Smith to have a 'better organized mind' than Brown (Turk and Kirkman
1989:19). According to the respondents in this experiment, low ratings
were given to Brown primarily because Brown's text is much less easy
to read than Smith's. This is not, however, because one text is more
'technical' than the other: both passages only use five technical words
and the information in each is presented in exactly the same sequence.
Turk and Kirkman conclude that the difference between the passages
can be found in the use of *non*-technical language: 'Smith's version is
readable because it is written in short sentences with direct active constructions. It avoids unfamiliar words, and inflated roundabout phrases.
Brown's version is difficult to read, with long sentences, long words, and
convoluted constructions' (Turk and Kirkman 1989:19). The problematic nature of these two passages—they are both factually 'correct' but
Smith's is preferred to Brown's for stylistic reasons—provides an example of one of the major issues that face all writers. If choices of style
can be as important as choices of content, how do you decide on the
right style? It is, therefore, particularly important for students, whether
writing in their first language or in a foreign language, to learn how to
establish an appropriate style for their particular writing purpose and
how to recognize and avoid 'inflated roundabout phrases' and 'convoluted constructions'.

Two major aspects of style are commonly dealt with (to a greater or
lesser extent) in most teaching materials. The first of these comes under
the broad heading 'formality'. The other is often discussed in terms of
'commitment' or *hedging*. Both are significant for the learner. Formality
can have a critical impact not only on how easy the text is to read, but
also on the way readers perceive their relationship with the writer. If
you make your text too formal or too informal for the context, readers
can feel either imposed upon or patronized. Issues of commitment and
hedging are central to the way in which writers signal their sense of
authority. Again, it is vitally important that writers are able to signal to
the reader where they stand in relation to what they are writing about.
It is easy to see how failure to do this in academic communication can
have serious consequences.

Formality

As we saw in **2.2** and **2.3**, certain written modes of expression have
achieved prestige in many societies, this prestige often being associated
with notions of formality. In the examples in Task 53, Brown, it might

be said, struck the wrong level of formality, which is why readers felt the text did not communicate successfully. Smith, on the other hand, did not try to appear too important or too authoritative, and succeeded in writing simply and directly. Fairclough has commented on the nature of formality thus:

> Formality is a common property in many societies of practices and discourses of high social prestige and restricted access. It is a contributory factor in keeping access restricted, for it makes demands on participants above and beyond those of most discourse, and the ability to meet those demands is itself unevenly distributed. It can also serve to generate awe among those who are excluded by it and daunted by it.
>
> (*Fairclough 1989:65*)

In such a context, it is perhaps not surprising that learners, and many experienced writers, often fail to achieve an appropriate degree of formality. When style is the only defence that the writer has from the comments of a potentially hostile readership, trying to sound more confident or important than you feel is a human enough thing to do.

  TASK 54

The following advice is given in a course book for students who have English as a first language. As this is the only advice on style in their unit on 'Essay writing', it might be helpful to extend the instructions. If you were to do so, what would you add? This could be either a comment or an activity.

A formal style and tone

The way we compose our sentences, the use of correct grammatical constructions, and appropriate vocabulary allows us to write in a formal style and convey a formal tone. In formal writing avoid:

colloquial words or expressions
slang
jargon
tautology
vague words or phrases
everyday similes, e.g. 'as white as a sheet', 'as black as thunder'.
Create your own vivid comparisons.

(*Hilton and Hyder 1992:172*)

Apprentice writers working in either their first or a foreign language might find Hilton and Hyder's advice a little difficult to follow. For example, learners frequently have problems in identifying what exactly 'vague words and phrases' are. We might note, too, that it is probably advisable to avoid tautology in any writing. A helpful addition to the advice given in the extract might be activities which encourage learners to investigate how degrees of formality and authority are constructed. For example, in English, students might consider how a variety of devices are used to create different degrees of distance between writers and readers. These will include obvious features such as forms of address (avoidance of first and second person in more formal texts, for example), and polite modality, but also less obvious ones such as differences between the noun phrase structure and the lexis of texts that show different degrees of formality (see the discussion of lexical density in **3.2**). As successful writers need to be able to make appropriate choices from the language system and to match their text to their readership in a way which ensures maximum impact, learners will need more examples than have been given in this extract, and also some opportunities for analysis.

 ## TASK 55

The activity below presents another approach to the explanation of formality in writing. What comments would you predict the author will make after the exercise? What approach to writing does the author appear to have adopted in preparing this exercise—**intellectual/rhetorical** or **social/genre**?

[NB *The example given here deals with only one of the pairs of texts mentioned in the instructions to students.*]

On the next two pages you will find two pairs of texts, each pair about the same subject. However, within each pair of texts you will find contrasting styles and effects—so different that they seem to belong to different worlds . . .

. . . The second pair are about a region in the Blue Mountains where people go bushwalking. The first piece will take you there along with the bushwalkers, while the second reads like an extract from a geography text book.

Check the details

When you look more closely you will see that the second piece is really a 'translation' or transformation of the first. See how many points they have in common.

The Kanangra Walls area

A

. . . The next day we set out from Dex Creek through a gently sloping area of short, dense scrub, with only our compasses to guide us. There were no tracks, only rabbit paths, so we had to make our way through a forest of waist-high bushes. Jenny's shins looked like the work of Jackson Pollock. Once through there, we discovered we were in the wrong place, and needed to do more bush-bashing to get to the western side of Moko Creek. We followed that ridge to the well-named Mount Strongleg.

To descend Strongleg buttress we had to drop 600 metres in about one and a half kilometres. It's spurs like this that made us think longingly of chairlifts and hang-gliders. But we managed the descent in about 50 minutes, and were glad to wallow in the Kanangra Creek. After a very long lunch we moved on downstream. Unfortunately the grassy banks of the Cox's river had been ripped out by a flood the previous August, so there was a lot of slow rock-scrambling. We stopped for the night on Kooriekirra Creek, and feasted on hot muffins and Stefan's delicious, pure Australian honey (not an advertisement) . . .

B

Below Kanangra Walls, the Gingerang Plateau stretches Northeast, and is drained by several creeks, including Dex Creek to the south, and Moko Creek to the north. The soil of the plateau is mostly sedimentary material. But it is exposed to all weather conditions, and only supports sclerophyll vegetation and acacia. The same vegetation extends along the ridges to Kooriekirra Top and, ultimately, Mt Strongleg.

The precipitous flanks of Mt Strongleg rise 600 metres above the Kanangra Creek. The peak forms one side of the northern end of the Kanangra Gorge, and it diverts the Kanangra Creek westwards before it can resume its northward course to the Cox's River. The steep descent of Kanangra Creek and others promotes a savage flow of water in the Cox's river. It can transport basalt boulders far down stream, which continually scours the banks of the river and modifies its course . . .

(Peters (ed.) 1989:27, 29)

The author comments as follows:

What's the same? Information on:
landmarks such as Dex Creek, Mogo Creek, Kanangra Creek, Cox's River, Mt Strongleg
the tough vegetation
the steepness of Mt Strongleg
large rocks in the bed of the Cox's River
changes in the profile of the Cox's River

What's different?
– A is a personal account from one of the walkers, hence "we". B is an impersonal account with no people in it at all.
– A takes you stage by stage on the walk. B presents things in relation to the two main geographical features of the area, Gingerang Plateau and Mt Strongleg.
– A takes the details of the landscape for granted. B adds in a lot of "hard" information about the landmarks and their orientation.

– A tells you what the walkers experience along the way. B gives you geological causes and effects.
– A uses everyday words and images such as "waist-high", "bush-bashing", "wallow", "ripped out", "feasted". B contains technical words, such as "drained", "sedimentary", "sclerophyl", "vegetation", "basalt".
– A's purpose is to entertain the reader. B's purpose is to explain the geography of the area.

(Peters (ed.) 1989:30)

Such an analysis can be helpful to learners in various ways, largely because it takes into account the significance of the social functions of language. By contextualizing the analysis in this way, the author has been able to provide an account of formality which makes the connection between contrasts in language use and the differing communicative purposes of two genres of writing. By means of this sort of analysis, learners can begin to see how communicative purpose and grammar combine to produce differences in style.

The above discussion clearly demonstrates the need that learners have for language system knowledge and context knowledge, and crucially the ability to make the relationship between them. Learners might have a large linguistic repertoire but not be able to implement this appropriately for particular contexts, or they may have a clear understanding of the need for different levels of formality but not have sufficient linguistic range to achieve the effects they desire. In the case of learners who neither have linguistic range nor an awareness of context, disaster looms at each moment they put pen to paper.

 ## TASK 56

The activity in Task 55 was designed for students who speak English as a first language. How might you wish to extend this explanation for foreign language learners?

The biggest problem for foreign language learners is likely to be that of language system knowledge. It would, for example, be possible to prepare activities to enable learners to study contrasts between the grammatical subjects of sentences in text A and text B, and also to identify differences in the structure of noun phrases. It would also be of interest, either with this example or with a collection of shorter texts, to explore the contention that 'passives are more common in formal writing'.

Hedging

A second major component of style in writing in academic settings is commitment or hedging. *Hedging* refers to the way in which a writer shows the extent to which he or she wishes to be responsible either for the accuracy of the ideas being put forward or for the ideas themselves.

Various ways of helping students understand this aspect of language use have been suggested.

▶ **TASK 57**

Two ways of dealing with commitment are exemplified below. Do you feel that they are similar or different? If they are different, then how would you describe this difference?

Extract 1

> 1 In the sentences below there are a number of examples of cautious language. Underline the appropriate words. If necessary refer to the Structure and Vocabulary Aid (page 67).
>
> **Adjusting to higher education**
>
> Other new students may refer to feelings of bewilderment because of the differences in size between school and a large university or poly-technic. . . . The sheer variety of possible activities can be confusing. . . . Students who have chosen to cater for themselves may, at first, have difficulty in finding time for shopping and housekeeping. . . .

(*Jordan 1992:64*)

Extract 2

> **Step 3**
>
> 5.5 Text 7.3 is a third version of the letter which mixes both per-sonal and impersonal styles. When the writer wishes to be accountable, this is made clear. Likewise, when the writer wishes to hedge, an impersonal style is used.
>
> Study Text 7.3 and list the ways in which the writer demon-strates accountability. Compare your rephrasing in Step 5.4 with the rephrasing in Text 7.3.

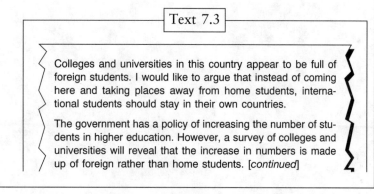

Text 7.3

> Colleges and universities in this country appear to be full of foreign students. I would like to argue that instead of coming here and taking places away from home students, interna-tional students should stay in their own countries.
>
> The government has a policy of increasing the number of stu-dents in higher education. However, a survey of colleges and universities will reveal that the increase in numbers is made up of foreign rather than home students. [*continued*]

(*White and McGovern 1994:63*)

Jordan has identified lexis as a major component of commitment, and in this and other exercises endeavours to increase the expressive range of learners by getting them to identify and use words and expressions that signal uncertainty or limited commitment. White and McGovern agree on the importance of signalling lexis. However, they also draw their readers' attention to the way in which writers can switch between personal and impersonal styles in order to increase or decrease their distance (and thence, their commitment) in relation to the ideas under discussion. This sets up interesting tensions between notions such as commitment and certainty. For example, it is possible to identify a phrase such as 'it appears to be' as a commitment-reducing statement about something that is uncertain, as the 'it' lessens the personal involvement of the writer. On the other hand, while 'it seems to me . . .' is equally uncertain, the use of the personal pronoun implies that the writer is, to some degree at least, committed to the statement.

9.7 Conclusion

In 9 we have considered the interaction of context, content, and communicative purpose from the point of view of writing for academic and study purposes. A significant part of our discussion has focused on the way in which different traditions in writing instruction can give contrasting insights into the nature of written language in these settings and provide learners with alternative ways of addressing the problem of how to become a writer in the context of study. We shall return to these questions in 11, when we shall see how different approaches to teaching writing influence the sorts of feedback that teachers give to learners.

10 Teaching writing skills

10.1 Introduction

In Section One we considered some of the factors, other than knowledge of the mechanics of writing and command of the language system, which can lead to successful writing. We saw that two of the most significant qualities associated with a person's capacity to write successfully are:

- the extent to which a writer is able to draw on a range of appropriate *processes* when he or she is engaged in the creation of written texts
- the extent of a writer's knowledge of the way in which context and content influence the *genres* of writing that are typical of particular communicative events.

In **8** and **9** we have considered issues related to context, content, and communicative purpose in the teaching of writing. In **10** we will look specifically at some of the ways in which writing processes and writing skills are treated in language teaching materials.

We saw in Section One that, while there have been many different descriptions of writing processes (see, for example, Hedge 1988; White and Arndt 1991; Harris 1993), there is a general consensus on the main elements. These are summarized in Figure 2 on page 39. As we have already discussed in **5.2**, the process of writing is not a simple linear progression. During each phase of the process writers may find themselves returning to an earlier phase in order to refine the meaning they are trying to develop. In this sense 'publishing' simply marks a point when the writer decides to stop writing. The text itself is never really 'finished'. In the rest of **10** we will consider the phases in this process.

10.2 Pre-writing

When Hedge talks about 'pre-writing' activities, she says that 'before putting pen to paper, the skilled writer in real life considers two important questions . . . What is the purpose of this piece of writing? . . . [and] . . . Who am I writing this for?' (Hedge 1988:21–2). These two questions relate closely to the discussion in **8** and **9** where we emphasized the importance of an understanding of the context and content of a text. Hedge also says that some pieces of writing require a great deal of preparation and that others can be written more or less spontaneously.

▶ TASK 58

What sort of pre-writing activity do you think experienced writers working in their first language would need to do before composing a text in the following contexts? Would they need to carry out research before starting to write, or would they be able to begin writing with a minimum of preparation, for example jotting down a list of points they wanted to cover?

1 Completing an application form for a course of study at a university
2 Writing a letter to a friend in another country in order to find out when it would be possible to visit them
3 Writing up the minutes of a committee meeting
4 Writing the instruction leaflet for a new microwave oven.

It is probable that context 4 will require the most pre-writing activity. In real life, the writer will have to talk to the engineers and designers who have developed the microwave oven, discuss food preparation techniques with food scientists, check on safety issues and how best to keep the oven clean, and so forth. Once all this information has been assembled, the writer will have to decide on an appropriate organizational framework for the text, check on any technical terms which have to be explained to the reader, and decide on what illustrations will be needed. The success or otherwise of the writer in this context will very much depend on their understanding of the constraints which the genre will impose on the text. For example, an instruction leaflet for a maintenance engineer will be radically different from the instruction leaflet for a domestic user. Using their knowledge of these differences, good technical writers can provide the right amount of the right information in a reader-friendly way. If the writer does not appreciate the nature of the genre, it will be difficult to ask the right sort of questions, include the right sort of information, and, in general, prepare a useful set of instructions.

An experienced writer would need to engage in less pre-writing activity to complete the other tasks. Some background knowledge of, for example, higher education institutions and their entry requirements will be required for context 1: if this is lacking, information will have to be sought from qualified informants or from reference books. The letter in context 2 probably needs no preparation at all—unless the writer decides to make a list of points to include. In 3, the only thing that an experienced writer might need to do is to check that he or she knows how to spell the names of the people who attended the meeting. He or she will probably already have knowledge of the appropriate form in which the minutes should be presented.

▶ TASK 59

In the following activity students are asked to prepare a tourist information broadsheet for their home town. How do the pre-writing tasks help them to develop writing skills? What is the teacher's role in this activity?

Procedure

Hold a group meeting to decide on the content of your sheet. During the meeting you must decide
- what information to include: local customs, best restaurants, etc.
- how to illustrate your broadsheet: maps, photographs, etc.
- who will do what: who will research the different sections, find the photographs, etc.

After a period of time your teacher will give you a chance to meet again to look at the information you have written and gathered. This time you should meet as a group to
- check that the information (and the English!) is accurate
- decide exactly what you will include
- produce your broadsheet.

MAKE SURE THAT THE INFORMATION IS CLEARLY AND EFFECTIVELY PRESENTED.

When you have finished you should display your work for the other members of the class.

Walk round and discuss each sheet.

(*Nolasco 1987:31*)

In this case the author has given learners very clear advice on how to work collaboratively in preparing the information sheet. Information gathering is presented as a shared task, as is the production of the broadsheet itself. So long as students have sufficient experience of the genre in question for them to be able both to identify what can be appropriately included in the target text, and to organize such a text, there can be significant advantages in providing this kind of framework for collaboration. In such a setting, the teacher has become a facilitator in this phase of the process, and well-managed class-work can make a strong contribution to the overall success of the writing activity. As Hedge says: 'Collaborative writing in the classroom generates discussions and activities which encourage an effective process of writing' (1988:12). Developing appropriate skills for the completion of pre-writing tasks can make an effective contribution in helping learners to become better writers.

▶ TASK 60

The following writing task is given after a series of activities in which students have been asked to investigate some of the linguistic features of 'instructions' (sequencing words, imperatives, impersonal / personal style). While the task provides the learner with some help in terms of language and context information, it offers little other support in preparing for the writing activity. What pre-writing activities could you ask your students to do in order to get the most from this exercise?

Writing activity

You are expecting an important American businessman to arrive at the airport in your country. He will need to know how to use a public telephone, so he can call you. Write a list of instructions. You will need words like these:

dial   (the disk with numbers 0–9)
receiver   (the thing you hold)
engaged   (when the person you call is already talking to someone)

(*Carrier 1981:43*)

Even though technological changes have made this particular task a little less valid than when the materials were first published, this sort of activity can still usefully be included in a teaching programme which covers writing instructions. By extending the range of tasks for students to do when preparing to write, the relevance of the task could be enhanced, or example, as follows:

Thinking about content
If you are concerned that your students will not want to write about telephones, one obvious way of modifying the task is to ask them to identify a piece of local technology that *would* be inaccessible to a visitor from the USA. This could then become the focus of the writing activity.

Thinking about the reader
The 'important American businessman' is an unfamiliar audience for students with little knowledge of the USA. Although he might be kept as an eventual reader, it may be more useful to assume other class members as immediate readers. For example the class might discuss what the American businessman would and would not know about the local technology, and draw up a needs profile which could be used at various stages of a writing process. The profile would make it possible to bring together the students' own knowledge of reader-writer relations in written instructions and their understanding of the gap between how things are done in their own country and how they are done elsewhere. This, in turn, would help with the planning and composing of the text. The profile could also be used by other class members in peer-evaluation

of first drafts of the instructions. Having an agreed evaluative frame-work makes it possible for one group to comment constructively on the work of other groups. Knowing that your peers will be evaluating your work provides a more motivating context in which to write than writing for an entirely fictitious reader.

Systematic preparation for writing

This kind of writing task requires research, in this case discovering any differences that exist between public telephones (or another bit of technology) in the USA and in the students' country. It would also be helpful to provide a procedure for data collection and for drafting and reviewing the instructions along the lines of the one described in Task 59.

Both the examples in Task 59 and in Task 60 require learners to write in relation to a set topic, something which takes a great deal of responsibility off the writer's shoulders. When learners have to take fuller responsibility for developing a text without a set theme, other techniques can be helpful. In such instances, an important part of pre-writing can involve what White and Arndt (1991:4) describe as 'generating', 'focusing', and 'structuring'.

Generating activities help learners find out what they want to write about and to overcome imaginative blocks. They can be helpful to writers working on their own, or they can be used with groups as a way of getting ideas moving before individual students then get on with composing. Generating activities can be extremely effective in language learning classrooms as they provide a practical purpose for discussion, and, by helping learners to share their experiences, can lead to increased motivation for individual writers.

Focusing activities help writers to identify priorities in what they have to say. Not only can such activities help writers to give emphasis to the most important parts of their argument, they can also assist in ensuring that what is being written about will be relevant to a potential reader.

Structuring activities help learners to review the way in which they are organizing their texts so that they will communicate effectively with potential readers.

▶ TASK 61

The three examples below represent activities that are commonly used to help learners with generating, structuring, and focusing. Study the examples and decide what the purpose of each activity is.

Example 1 (Mind map)

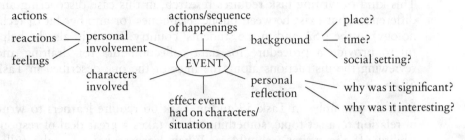

You have been asked to write an account of a personal experience.

1 Talk about various elements which might be included in an account of a personal experience. Note down the results of your discussion in a mind map. (It might look a little like the one given here.)

2 Select a personal experience that you would like to write about. Use your mind map to decide which elements will be the most interesting or significant for the particular experience you plan to describe.

(adapted from White and Arndt 1991:63–4)

Example 2 (Prioritizing lists)

GETTING YOUR IDEAS INTO ORDER

This is something you could do after brainstorming, speed writing, or 'wh' questions.
– Look through your notes.
– Use numbers or arrows to put them in the order you want to mention them in writing.
e.g. Ordering notes in preparation for a job application letter:

Assistant Chef – Advertiser Sat 11th July
③ Asian cooking is my specialty
② 2 years experience in America
④ Prefer part-time work but f/t is ok
⑥ Close to home
⑤ Don't mind split shifts
① 3 year certificate course

(Brown and Hood 1989:10)

Example 3 (Picture prompts)

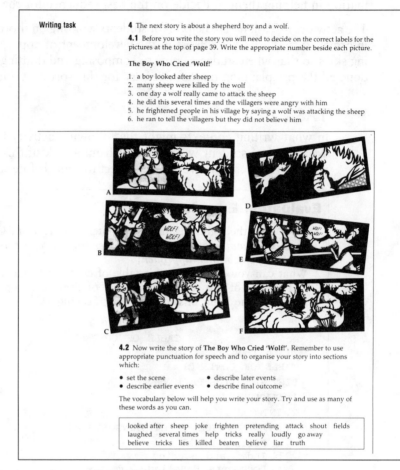

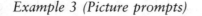

(*Hopkins and Tribble 1989:38–9*)

Example 1, the mind map, demonstrates a technique which can help writers to generate ideas and also to focus them. The visual nature of the mind map is particularly useful in class or group work where a board or flip-chart can be used as a way of building a consensual view of a problem or set of issues, and then identifying relationships between different aspects of the problem and selecting those elements which it will be useful to write about.

In contrast, Examples 2 and 3 are essentially single function activities. Example 2 shows how a listing of information can be used to prioritize and select what to write about—a focusing activity. Example 3 is for students at an earlier point in language learning. A great deal of the content of the story they are to write has been provided, thereby avoiding problems in generating and focusing ideas. This task focuses on problems of structuring the text. The authors have presented a generic structure for this type of narrative and the learners are asked to use this information in helping them to decide on the best sequence for the narrative.

The activities in Task 61 are helpful for students working on short, relatively informal texts. They would assist in the development of appropriate writing skills so that when students come to composing and drafting they have done all the pre-planning that is necessary for this sort of writing.

▶ # TASK 62

In what writing contexts might the following activity be helpful? What type of student would benefit from a task of this kind, and what sorts of activities would you expect to come before such a task?

Evaluation Exercise 3

1 How does the following table of contents differ from Gregory's? [*another example of the contents pages from a report using a different organizational approach*]
2 What can you learn from this table of contents about the report?
      The title of the report is 'Review of Present Company Filing System in the Light of Modern Filing Techniques'.

```
                    TABLE OF CONTENTS                    71
     TITLE PAGE                                        (i)
     TABLE OF CONTENTS                                 (ii)
     LIST OF ILLUSTRATIONS                             (iii)
     1. SUMMARY                                        1
     2. INTRODUCTION                                   2
     3. INVESTIGATION OF EXISTING SYSTEM               3
        a. Filing Manual
        b. Index and Sorting
        c. Documents Handling / Retrieving
        d. Physical Condition:
             (i) Equipment Sizes
            (ii) Office Facilities
     4. DISADVANTAGES OF SYSTEM                         15
        a. Location
        b. Management Needs
     5. PRELIMINARY OVERVIEW OF NEW SYSTEMS             17
        a. Full Computerization
             (i) Advantages
            (ii) Setbacks
                  - Complexity
                  - Training
        b. Semi-computerization
             (i) Advantages
            (ii) Impact on Company Documentation
     6. CONCLUSION                                      24
     7. RECOMMENDATIONS                                 27
```

(*Doherty, Knapp, and Swift 1987:132*)

This exercise is one of a series designed to help learners write better business reports—a task for upper intermediate or advanced students with a real-world need to write such documents. At this point in a cycle of activities, the contents page of the report is being focused on because it represents a key to the planning processes which went into the preparation of the report itself. In earlier sections, the authors stress the need to establish what the focus of the report should be and how to help the reader to see relationships between its different components. In this stage in the programme of instruction they are asking learners to consider the different merits of various approaches to the presentation of information in a report, and are also reviewing the planning processes that were gone through in order to develop the text. They attempt to get round some of the methodological problems of helping students understand how this sort of planning is done by creating a dialogue between an 'expert' writer (GJ) and a colleague (FR):

> FR . . . and from the body, you work towards the conclusions and then the recommendations?
>
> GJ Precisely, but I need to introduce these three sections so I write an introduction. But, being a reader of reports as well as a writer, I am well aware that most readers of this report will only look at the summary. So, I place a summary before the introduction, which, in fact, summarizes the four major parts. So my first section is:
> – a summary of the introduction
> – a summary of the body
> – a summary of the conclusions
> – a summary of the recommendations.
> But I don't give these subheadings, I simply place all this information under the one heading: Summary.

(Doherty, Knapp, and Swift 1987:130)

In effect, Doherty *et al.* are synthesizing a view of best practice as established through protocol studies such as those discussed in **5.3**. They then present this view of a writing process to learners—first to investigate and then to consider as a possible basis for their own writing practice. Such an approach to preparing for writing reduces the emphasis on the actual composition, stressing rather the importance of good preparation. If writers have a clear sense of direction, based on an explicit understanding of the structure of the text they are going to write and on the preparation they have carried out in the context of this understanding, composition itself can cease to be dependent on invention alone and become much more a process of systematic assembly.

In this review of writing processes, we have now moved from the generation, collection, and organizing of ideas, through planning of extended texts, to a point in the cycle where the writer has put pen to paper, or fingers to keyboard.

10.3 Composing and drafting

As indicated in Figure 2 (page 32), there is never a simple cut-off point between pre-writing and composing—there always remains an inevitable to-ing and fro-ing between the two activities. However, there does need to be some point at which the writer begins to 'translate plans and ideas into provisional text' (Harris 1993:55) and moves from thinking about writing to doing it. This is called variously 'composing' (Hedge 1988), 'drafting' (White and Arndt 1991), or 'creating and developing' (Harris 1993). During composing, writers move towards a text that most closely matches what they want to convey to their reader.

Brown and Hood (1989) give the following exercise to help bring students to the point of composing. In Stage 1, groups of students are given a headline as an aid to the generation of ideas, along with a set of focusing questions commonly used by journalists—who? where? when? what? In this way, they are provided with assistance in generating ideas, focusing, and structuring. In Stage 2, students work individually to prepare short newspaper articles which draw on this initial phase.

Stage 1

Lost boys found

who?   2 boys, aged 10 and 12

where?   in the bush, in the Dandenong Ranges, near Melbourne

when?   lost yesterday. Found this morning

what?   wandered away from a family picnic

Two boys, aged 10 and 12, who wandered away from a family picnic in the Dandenong Ranges near Melbourne yesterday, were found this morning after spending all night in the bush.

Stage 2

Lost boys found

who?

where?

when?

what?

(*Brown and Hood 1989:128*)

Once they have overcome the problem of getting started, students are then asked to continue writing and to provide more detail on different aspects of the story. The same four questions can be used to generate more ideas for the text which follows on from this opening. The task is designed for intermediate students and results in what is still a relatively simple text.

▶ **TASK 63**

In the context of a longer essay, how could you adapt such an approach in order to help learners overcome temporary blocks that they might meet while composing? What other question words might be useful, for example, or in what other ways might a writer attempt to create a 'dialogue' with a possible reader?

At a general level, the key would seem to be to ask yourself if the reader is being asked to make unreasonable 'jumps' in order to follow the logic of what you are saying. In other words, are you assuming that your reader can follow a thread of argument that you have been living with intimately for some time, but which is entirely new to them? More specifically, White (1987) presents an activity which is in some senses analogous to that proposed by Brown and Hood. This activity is designed to help a writer make the transition from ideas-generating to composing in a more advanced setting, and uses a mnemonic to help students produce ideas which can eventually be incorporated into composition:

A Associate the theme with something else
D Define it
A Apply the idea
D Describe it
C Compare it with something else
A Argue for or against the subject
N Narrate the development or history of it

This yields the mnemonic:

A DAD CAN

You can use this mnemonic to recall idea-generating processes when you are trying to produce ideas for a writing assignment.

(*White 1987:55*)

Following this activity, White goes on to present a theme for learners to work with—'The will to learn'—and then takes students through a series of activities which lead to the writing of a first draft:

Producing ideas
Organizing ideas
Developing a theme
Evolving a plan
Taking audience into account
Getting started

Given the number of stages which White and other authors recommend in the process of getting ready to compose, it seems that tasks which require students to jump immediately into composition are courting a high risk of failure. This being said, it is worth bearing in mind that White may be *too* specific—even inflexible—in proposing this sort of mnemonic. Writers have many different dispositions and cognitive styles, and teachers must always recognize that there will be many ways at arriving at a successful piece of writing, some of which will be decidedly idiosyncratic.

▶ TASK 64

The following exercise asks the student writer to embark on composition with no other direct preparation. Do you think any preparation is necessary to complete this task, and if so, what?

Writing Tasks

1 Write a pamphlet outlining the jobs of a customs officer. You should state what you think his obligations are. The pamphlet will be used to try and recruit people into the work force of the Customs and Excise Department.

(*Arnold and Harmer 1978:48*)

In the light of our earlier discussions, it is probable that we would encourage students to undertake a range of preparatory activities in order to find out about customs officers and recruitment pamphlets before asking them to write such a text. We would also try to set up a readership other than an evaluating teacher for the text they produced.

The point to underline here is that it is probably not helpful to treat composition as an isolated activity. While it may be a distinct stage in the writing process, 'composition' is only one part of a cycle, and the moment when pen touches paper for the first time is, in many cases, not the moment when composition begins. In most cases, successful composing only happens after a writer has built up an extensive experience of written texts, has developed a range of skills as a writer, and has then done work in specific preparation for the text in hand. Both long-term and immediate preparation supports writers during composition and makes it possible for them to monitor and evaluate what they are writing at the moment of production. Composing is thus a series of moments in which writers are in dynamic interaction with:

- the argument they are trying to develop or the perception they are trying to share
- their understanding of the expectations of their probable reader
- their appreciation of all the other similar texts that precede the one they are currently composing.

10.4 Revising and editing

Composing and drafting do not usually mark the end point of the writing process. At the very least, writers are continuously reading through what they have written and making corrections to ensure both clarity of expression and factual and grammatical accuracy. In fact, in most instances of extended writing, it is common for more than one cycle of revision and editing to take place before a 'final' piece of writing is produced. This book will have gone through five or six before it is finished!

Hedge (1988:23) expresses an opinion which is shared by most commentators on the teaching of writing when she says: 'Good writers tend to concentrate on getting the content right first and leave details like correcting spelling, punctuation and grammar until later.' 'Getting the content right' is a reasonable summary of what should happen during *revision*. The rest is *editing*. In this sense, revision is therefore incorporated into the writing process and is very different from what often happens to the first drafts of student writing. Think of the cases when learners hand in first drafts as if they were finished texts and teachers arrive at a 'mark' for these texts by counting mistakes. Students require a checklist of guidelines which will make it possible for them to edit their work. They also need to realize that revising and editing is an integral part of the process of writing, and not something that can be tacked on as an optional extra.

There are several examples of editing checklists in published materials. Hedge, for instance, suggests that writers should ask themselves the following questions both during and after composition:

- Am I sharing my impressions clearly enough with my reader?
- Have I missed out any important points of information?
- Are there any points in the writing where my reader has to make a 'jump' because I've omitted a line of argument or I've forgotten to explain something?
- Does the vocabulary need to be made stronger at any point?
- Are there any sentences which don't say much or which are too repetitive and could be missed out?
- Can I rearrange any sets of sentences to make the writing clearer or more interesting?
- Do I need to rearrange any paragraphs?
- Are the links between sections clear? Do they guide my reader through the writing?

(*Hedge 1988:23*)

Hopkins and Tribble provide the following checklist for elementary writers:

Improving your writing
First check   Check that your writing makes sense
              Is it correctly organized on the page?
              Is the information presented in a clear, logical order?
              Have you put in all the information your reader needs?
              Have you put in unnecessary information?

(*Adapted from Hopkins and Tribble 1989:10*)

 ## TASK 65

Consider the groups of more advanced writers who need to write particular kinds of texts (for example, laboratory reports, business reports, academic essays and articles). Choose one such group and decide what should be covered by a revision checklist for them.

The checklist approach is also useful when it comes to the last part of a writing cycle, editing. Even with the editing stage, however, finality should never be assumed! As Harris (1993) says, there is always a need for 'reading back over the text so far developed—whether this is only part of a draft of a full draft . . . to ensure that the text is maintaining an overall *coherence*. Poor writers . . . rarely review or scan back even when a draft is finished' (Harris 1993:62).

TASK 66

If a revising checklist covers areas such as appropriate organization, clarity of expression and the sufficiency and relevance of information, what would you consider important to include in a checklist for the final editing of a draft?

Editing checklists may well vary from situation to situation, making it possible to focus on different aspects of language system knowledge. You may want beginners from certain language backgrounds to pay particular attention to well known problems in grammar—prepositions or articles being obvious candidates. In other contexts you may wish to provide a more general set of instructions such as those presented by Nolasco which conflate *revising* and *editing*.

The procedure you use when you reread a final draft is very personal, but it is important to be systematic. We need to check:

the order in which the information is presented (is it clear, logical and effective?)
the layout
the spelling
punctuation
handwriting
word order
choice of words
grammar (especially the form and choice of tenses)

(*Nolasco 1987:31*)

▶ TASK 67

Consider groups of advanced learners you have taught—or even think about your own needs as a writer. What types of editing checklists might be helpful to them or to you?

10.5 Conclusion

In 10 we have considered some of the ways in which teaching materials can help learners to enhance their awareness of the processes associated with successful writing and to improve their skills as writers. We have also reviewed some of the ways in which an understanding of genre—the demands of the context of writing—influence both the sorts of process that a writer may choose in order to approach a writing task and the way that they go about completing that task. In 11 we will draw together our discussion of different approaches to the teaching of writing by looking at a range of options that are available to teachers when responding to student writing.

11 Responding to student writing

11.1 Introduction

We have seen how different approaches to the teaching of writing can require different types of response from the teacher. In **11** we will consider a range of possible responses to student writing, and the different pedagogic objectives which motivate them. During this discussion we will take into account the different reasons that learners have for writing and the different roles that teachers can take on when they respond to texts that students have written.

▶ **TASK 68**

In **7** we discussed the difference between activities that are intended to help students *learn to write* and to *write to learn*. Will there be a significant difference between the way a teacher responds to texts that have been written with these two contrasting purposes?

In **7** we used an activity from the *New Cambridge English Course* as an example of a *writing to learn* task (see Example 3 in Task 41).

A typical way of marking writing done in response to such a task would be:

> *are*
> 1. There is some children in the room. ✗
>
> 2. There are some chairs in the room. ✓
>
> 3. There is a light on the table. ✓
>
> *some*
> 4. There are ∧ children in the room. ✗

In *writing to learn* activities, learners usually want clear, unambiguous feedback on the language they have used; they want to know if they are right or wrong so that they can learn from their mistakes. This can apply equally to sentence-level tasks such as the one above, and to quite extensive pieces of writing where the teacher and learner have agreed that the main purpose of the task is to practise the target language in a controlled way.

In *learning to write* activities, however, this approach to marking is not likely to be appropriate. This is because, as we have seen, writing is such a complex, multi-faceted activity that teachers have to respond to learners' many needs by taking on a variety of roles—not simply that of judge of whether a sentence is 'right' or 'wrong'.

 ## TASK 69

Think about the different aspects of a text that teachers evaluate when marking student writing, and the different points of view they can take in order to make evaluations. What roles do teachers typically take on when they are readers of student writing?

Let us now look at four basic roles which are available for teachers as readers. We will call them *audience*, *assistant*, *evaluator*, and *examiner*. A teacher can take on these roles at different stages in the writing cycle.

11.2 Four basic roles

As audience, teachers have the same sorts of responsibilities and concerns as any reader. For example, is the text interesting? Is it easy to understand? Does it tell us about the writer and the writer's view of the world? This is something that we can forget as we busy ourselves in our search for mistakes or infelicities, with the risk that our students may feel that we have denied the value of what they have to say. Part of our responsibility to our students is, therefore, to respond to the ideas, feelings, or perceptions that they have tried to communicate through their writing.

As assistants, teachers work with learners to make sure that the text is as effective as possible in relation to its purpose. While working as an assistant, the teacher sees the writing as work in progress and helps learners to use or to extend their knowledge of the best way of going about writing the text, the language appropriate to the task, the genre in which they are writing, and, if necessary, the subject-matter of the text.

As evaluators, teachers are no longer trying to improve a particular text. Rather they are commenting on the learners' overall performance and strengths and weaknesses with the aim of helping them write more effectively in the future. Evaluation is done once a piece of writing is considered to be 'finished', although it might also be done at the end of a course in order to guide learners towards programmes which will help them continue to develop as writers. Evaluation can also give an indication of a learner's effectiveness as a writer which other teachers can use when the learner joins a new course.

As examiners, teachers take on yet another role. They have to provide as objective an assessment as possible of how well a student can write, on the basis of work written within the constraints of a formal examination, or that of a portfolio of work that has been accumulated over a period of time. This assessment usually has to be based on explicit criteria and be replicable by another trained examiner. The grade that is given is often also intended to help another educational institution, or a prospective employer, understand what the candidate can and cannot do as a writer.

▶ **TASK 70**

Below is an example of student writing and a response to the text. Do you recognize this as a common way of responding to student writing? Whcih for the four roles described above do you feel the teacher has taken on in this instance, and what are the advantages or disadvantages of such a response?

MY EARLIEST MEMORIES

My earliest memories are ~~very niceand~~ important to me. I was borne~~d~~ in Genoa, but when I was two years old my

p ~~P~~arents went to live in Sondrio, a quiet town in the ~~hight~~ *high* Lombardia near the Swiss border.

I lived there / *for* ten years, ten beautiful years. I'd like to remember the <u>hight</u> mountains around the town, the <u>blou</u> *blue* sky, the clean air and the snow, the friends.

peace?   *?*
That <u>quiet</u> has been very important for my <u>mind</u> and for my character.

so   *from*
I remember <u>too</u> many things <u>of</u> that period which I can't forget. Also now, that I live in Genoa and in Milan I try to go to Sondrio *often* as ~~soon~~ as possible every week, because <u>there</u> I've a lot of friends.

A good effort! B-

This way of marking writing is something that will be familiar to most of us. Think about writing tasks you have done as a learner of a foreign language. As we saw in Task 68, such a focus on correction is appropriate as a way of responding to a *writing to learn* exercise. It is less appropriate in this instance, however, for although it deals with some sentence-level problems, it fails to address other difficulties that are raised by the text, for example paragraph organization or the extent to which the writer is saying enough to satisfy the reader. Also, the comments that the teacher gives at the end of the text raise other difficulties. What does 'A good effort' mean? Does 'B–' refer to the number of mistakes made, the effort of the writer, or the performance of other students in the class?

What the teacher seems to be doing in giving this response is to try to play at least three roles at the same time—with only limited success in any of them. By devoting time to identifying problems in the learner's control of the language system the teacher has tried to *assist* the learner to make improvements in the text. However, the comments cannot in fact help the learner to improve *this* text as it is already complete; it has gone past the point when improvement is permitted. By giving a final *evaluative* comment the teacher might be wishing to encourage the learner and to point them in the right direction for future writing, but the comment is too vague to be useful. By giving a grade of B– (one assumes a fairly weak grade) the teacher is moving towards the role of *examiner* and is indicating that the text has failed to achieve excellence. Finally, the teacher has failed to give any indication of whether or not they enjoyed reading the text and found it gave an insight into their student's experience of the world. In other words, they have avoided the role of *audience*.

Marking student writing in this way has been subject to criticism:

> . . . the teacher's response is to the finished product. The teacher can only judge and evaluate, not influence the piece of writing. Responding to a paper only at the end limits us to doing the following:
>
> 1 giving the paper a grade (A, B, C or 70, 80, 90 etc.);
> 2 writing a comment: very good, needs improvement, careless;
> 3 correcting errors.

> If we sometimes feel the futility of this enterprise, let us put ourselves in the position of a student who has worked hard on a composition, looking up words in the dictionary, rereading, and checking. When he gets his paper back it looks like this . . .

> . . . What is the student to do now? What he does, of course, quite often is to groan, put the paper away, and hope he'll somehow get fewer 'red marks' next time.

(*Raimes 1983:139–41*)

One way out of this difficulty would seem to be **not** to wait until a text has been finished to make comments on it. Once the text has been handed in it is impossible to help the reader improve it!

Raimes provides two charts which summarize the contrast between two different types of feedback: feedback you can give once a text is thought to be 'finished', and comments which are made on a text during the process of writing. The first chart, Cycle A, describes what Raimes calls a typical classroom writing cycle in which the teacher's main responsibility is to set a topic and then to assess the results of the student's effort.

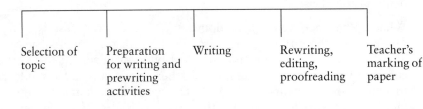

Selection of topic   Preparation for writing and prewriting activities   Writing   Rewriting, editing, proofreading   Teacher's marking of paper

(*Raimes 1983:139*)

Such a procedure tends to produce feedback like the example in Task 70. If the task has not been clearly specified and if neither student nor teacher really understands why the writing is being done, this sort of marking can be depressingly time-consuming for the teacher and demotivating for the learner.

The second pattern, Cycle B (opposite), shows a sequence of classroom activities which Raimes considers to have a greater potential for providing the learner with constructive feedback. In this model there is, clearly, scope for a range of different types of comment, each of which will be appropriate for a particular moment in the development of the text—with the majority of feedback being provided well before the text is handed in for any form of final assessment. Indeed, in this model the final evaluation refers to 'progress from draft 1 to draft 3' rather than any judgement on the end product of the writing process.

The main problem with the comments on the student text given earlier, therefore, is that they were made too late. What we need are strategies that make it possible to give constructive comments on drafts of student writing rather than waiting until the text is deemed to be finished. If this can be done effectively, by the time a text is handed in for a final evaluation most of the problems that the writer might have had should have been eliminated. Such strategies will also help us to separate the different roles of the 'teacher as reader' from each other, ensuring that when we respond to learner writing our students understand the purpose of our comments at each stage. We will now consider ways of responding to learner writing that are appropriate to these different roles.

Selection of topic by teacher and/or students → Preparation for writing/ prewriting activities → Teacher reads notes, lists, outlines, etc. and makes suggestions → Student writes draft 1 → Student makes outline of draft 1 → Teacher and students read draft: add comments and suggestions about content → Student writes draft 2 → Student reads draft 2 with guidelines or checklist: makes changes → Teacher reads draft 2: indicates good points and areas for improvement → Student writes draft 3 → Student edits and proofreads → Teacher evaluates progress from draft 1 to draft 3 → Teacher assigns follow-up tasks to help in weak areas

(Raimes 1983:140–1)

11.3　Audience

White and Arndt give the following guideline for responding to student writing: 'Respond as a genuine and interested reader rather than as a judge and evaluator' (White and Arndt 1991:125). They then give an example of the sort of response which they feel is most effective (to a text with the title 'My most unforgettable character'):

1. I really appreciate your sharing this experience with me. I found your story to be a touching piece of writing.
2. The first two paragraphs could be made more interesting for the reader. How?
3. Try changing the order of events and paragraphs . . .

(*White and Arndt 1991:128*)

▶　TASK 71

This particular style may not suit all teachers, but there are many ways of formulating your response. Raimes gives the following example of a short text. Taking the role of *audience*, what kind of comment would you make on this text?

My family is a large family, having six people live together in the house. Each one has different way to help them relax. An also the way they thought is relaxing, having give me too much angry.

For example, my youngest sister is love chinese music, therefor whenever she at home do her homework always has the music on. That bother me a lot. Because she and I live in the same room making me have to stop with the arcurment with her.

But the most angry is get up in the morning with a disco music. That rely make me crazy. That whole day I just have bad feeling. That is my youngest brother relax's way.

(*Raimes 1983:140–1*)

Raimes formulates her own response in the following way:

You have told us about two members of your family. Now I am wondering what the others do to relax! Do they like music too?

(*Raimes 1983:142*)

In this instance the student is left in no doubt that the teacher has been interested in the text they have been reading and has understood the content of what is being said. Her comments and questions invite the learner to expand the text and build upon what has been written already.

11.4 Assistant

We have seen that the process of writing—especially of writing more extended texts—typically comprises cycles of preparation, composition, revising, and editing. The teacher can assist the learner at each point in the cycle, or make sure that someone else (for example a fellow student) will take responsibility for working with the writer to make the text as clear and effective as possible. This is an important point, as one of the most significant contributions that a teacher can make in the writing classroom is to create a community of *readers* as well as a community of *writers*. If this is done consistently and thoroughly, teachers will find that their workload can often be significantly reduced rather than increased!

▶ TASK 72

Three of the stages involved in writing a text are given below. What practical steps can a teacher take:

1 To respond to the writing that students are doing during this process?
2 To make sure that *someone* has read and responded to this writing?

Preparation
First draft
Subsequent drafts

Four practical techniques which can increase a teacher's opportunities to read drafts of student writing are described below.

1 Conferencing
Teachers can be more easily involved in the preparation stage of writing if class time is used for this. One way of achieving this is called 'conferencing'. In a conferencing session which focuses on plans and first drafts, the teacher might initially work with the whole class to set up a writing activity—factual writing is often best suited to this type of approach. It can be any activity that is relevant to the needs of the learners, for example a commentary on statistics or tables, a report on an experimental procedure, or a review of a literary work. The essentials of the technique are (assuming a session of 90 minutes):

30 minutes
1 Set a writing task, giving time for class discussion to clarify any difficulties and/or to establish a consensus on the objectives of the piece of writing.
2 Provide guidelines for the writing task.
3 Get students to work in pairs to discuss language issues related to the task and the content of the texts they will write.
4 Have a short feedback session to clear up any problems that students might encounter with the task.

60 minutes

5 Set students to write individually for the rest of the lesson.
6 Begin to conference with individual students ten minutes after writing has started. With up to 20 students it should be possible to have two- or three-minute conferences with each student during the remaining hour. In a class of more than 20 learners it will be necessary to have some or all of this discussion with pairs.

Although conferencing requires the teacher to do a lot of moving around, the results that can be obtained from individual discussion are very rewarding. Clearly, the technique need not be restricted to the discussion of first drafts, but can be used at any time during the development of a text. The major problem the teacher faces in using it is to ensure that the rest of the class is working effectively while the conferencing sessions are going on. However, the benefits are usually so tangible that many teachers (especially in higher education) allocate at least one session a term for brief one-to-one conferences with each student in the class.

 ## TASK 73

How far do you think conferencing activities of this kind would be appropriate in a classroom context that you are familiar with?

2 Group writing
In the following activity, Hedge gives another useful example of how to maximize the opportunities for commenting on a text at the planning and draft stages.

	4.5 Writing in a group
LEVEL	**Lower intermediate to advanced**
TOPIC	**A story or description**
IN CLASS	1 Prepare a piece of writing with your class in the normal way. A story or description, e.g. of a festival, are the best types of text to prepare as these lend themselves to group writing.
	2 Explain to your students that they are going to do this piece of writing in a group, planning together, writing a section each, and checking each other's drafts.
	3 Organize your students into groups of four or five and appoint a group leader whose role is to get things started and to direct discussion.
	4 Each group decides how to organize the writing, what the order of events (or parts of the description) will be, and how many paragraphs to write. Each student is to write one section.
	5 When the various parts are completed, students exchange their work with other members of the group and mark the drafts for revision. They could be given a marking code like the one in the introduction to this section.

6 Students then redraft their work.

7 The various pieces can then be assembled and changes made to them to ensure coherence between them, such as careful use of time adverbials in a story.

REMARKS This activity has advantages for both the teacher and the students. The teacher has six rather than thirty pieces of writing to monitor and assist with and can spend more time on the final drafts. The students gain help from each other in planning and drafting, and obtain experience in identifying problems in writing. Discussion by several people means that more ideas and improvements are applied to a piece of writing and the discussion itself can constitute natural fluency practice.

(*Hedge 1988:157–8*)

▶ TASK 74

Would you be able to follow this set of instructions with the kinds of groups you teach or have taught? What local circumstances might prevent an implementation of these ideas?

Such an activity requires a degree of learner training if it is to work effectively and, as Hedge comments, is best for certain types of writing. However, the principle of encouraging students to become informed readers of one another's writing is an important one.

3 Reformulating

Reformulating a text is another way of providing feedback to students after a first draft has been written. This technique was first proposed by Andrew Cohen (Cohen 1983), and has since been developed by other teachers (Allwright et al. 1988; Tribble 1990). The teacher explains what the reformulation procedure will entail, and then students and teacher agree on a topic and students prepare a first draft. The teacher takes in the first drafts but does not mark them. All he or she does at this stage is to select a text which displays problems that other members of the group will benefit from studying. This text can be retyped to help preserve the anonymity of the writer. The next stage is best done by a colleague of the teacher's. (If the students are working in a specialist area such as medicine or physics, the reformulating may be done by a colleague from the relevant department.) The colleague rewrites the selected text as sympathetically as possible, not changing its content or argumentation. Rather, it is re-worded so that it most closely approximates what a competent writer *would have written*. This reformulated text and the original student draft are then available for group discussion.

An example of the beginning of a student text and a reformulation are given below.

Student text

THE BANISHMENT OF FOREIGNERS

1 INTRODUCTION

States banish unwanted foreigners almost daily. It is still not a very common matter taking into account the great number of foreigners. Only citizens have full protection against expulsion. Some foreigners are still better protected against returning than others are. The protection is based on international law.

2 LEGAL BACKGROUND

In principle an independent state is the highest unit of human society. There is no higher body which can rule over a sovereign state without its consent. However, due to practical needs there has been developed special rules concerning the behaviour of states. Without these rules peaceful coexistence between states would hardly have been possible. These rules are called '(public) international law'.

Reformulation

THE BANISHMENT OF FOREIGNERS

1 INTRODUCTION

Sovereign states banish foreigners whom they consider undesirable almost daily, yet it is still not a very common occurrence given the large number of foreign residents in most states. While only citizens have full protection against expulsion, some foreigners are better protected than others as a result of international law.

2 LEGAL BACKGROUND

In principle an independent state is the highest administrative unit in human society and no body can have juristiction over this state without its consent. However, as a response to practical needs special rules have developed concerning the behaviour states which are essential to their peaceful coexistence. These rules are called '(public) international law'.

▶ TASK 75

What differences do you notice between the two versions of this text? How might you exploit them in classroom discussion? What disadvantages, if any, do you see in such a procedure?

These texts can be worked with in many different ways, depending on the needs of the group. As Hedge says:

The advantages of reformulation are several. It enables students to see a 'native speaker' or 'proficient writer' model with which to compare their own attempts. It encourages students to discuss issues concerning organization, the development of ideas, the writer's sense of audience, and appropriate style. These important issues are often neglected in correction activities.

(*Hedge 1988:159–60*)

4 Peer editing

In peer editing learners work together to develop drafts before the teacher sees them. They need to recognize the roles that they are taking on in responding to texts that have been written by fellow students. This requires training and support in the early stages, but as learners become more confident they are able to see the benefits of this way of working. Students are quick to recognize that their peers can see problems in their texts more easily than they can themselves. White and Arndt give a useful example of a cycle of activities for peer editing:

Materials   **Students' own draft texts**

Procedure   1 Have students work with a partner, and get each to read what the other has drafted so far. They should make notes of places in their partner's draft:

– that they particularly liked or enjoyed
– that they particularly disliked or found unnecessary
– that they found unclear
– that they would have liked to know more about

Lastly, they should summarise their partner's text: *The main idea in this paper is . . .*

2 They now return their papers to each other and discuss the summary and the points that they have noted, beginning with the good points and going on to the things that need clarifying or improving. In the process, they should try to jointly improve what they have written.

(*White and Arndt 1991:130*)

This application of peer editing focuses on the message that the writer is developing. Other peer editing sessions could make use of revision or editing checklists such as those discussed in **10.4**.

11.5 Evaluator

Although the whole process of draft improvement involves evaluations of one kind or another, the evaluation of a finished text is of a different order of importance as it often contributes to a grade that the learner will receive at the end of a teaching programme. It becomes an evaluation not just of the text but also of the learner.

 TASK 76

A piece of writing provides a variety of data, for example evidence of the learner's control of the grammatical system of the language and evidence of their range of vocabulary knowledge. It can also perform various functions, for example persuading, entertaining, and informing, as well as giving us some sense of what sort of a person the writer is and how he or she sees the world. If evaluative comments such as 'Good effort!' or 'Some interesting ideas but a little unclear in places. Be careful with your use of articles', give little satisfaction to teachers and learners alike, how can teachers provide more effective evaluation?

One approach to evaluation that has been widely adopted over recent years (see Carroll and West 1989) makes use of *multiple* yardsticks, so that a text is not assessed on a single dimension but is viewed as being the result of a complex of different skills and knowledge, each of which makes a significant contribution to the development of the whole.

An example of such an evaluative checklist is given below. This has been adapted by the author for use with adult learners on a report-writing course. It was originally developed by a group of teachers working in secondary schools in Austria to provide a common evaluative framework in their school system. Five major aspects of a piece of written work are evaluated and each of these aspects is accompanied by explicit descriptors of what is meant by the different band-scales. A range of possible scores is given for each band. These scores can be converted into an overall grade.

Assessment scale for written work

scores 8 or above	A	≥ 90% = 9	≥ 50% = 5
scores 6 to 7	B	≥ 80% = 8	≥ 40% = 4
scores 4 to 5	C	≥ 70% = 7	≥ 30% = 3
scores 2 to 3	D	≥ 60% = 6	≥ 20% = 2
scores 0 to 1	F		

Area	Score	Descriptor
Task Fulfilment/ Content	20–17	**Excellent to very good:** Excellent to very good treatment of the subject; considerable variety of ideas or argument; independent and thorough interpretation of the topic; content relevant to the topic; accurate detail
	16–12	**Good to average:** Adequate treatment of topic; some variety of ideas or argument; some independence of interpretation of the topic; most content relevant to the topic; reasonably accurate detail
	11–8	**Fair to Poor:** Treatment of the topic is hardly adequate; little variety of ideas or argument; some irrelevant content; lacking detail
	7–5	**Very Poor:** Inadequate treatment of the topic; no variety of ideas or argument; content irrelevant, or very restricted; almost no useful detail
	4–0	**Inadequate:** Fails to address the task with any effectiveness
Organization	20–17	**Excellent to very good:** Fluent expression, ideas clearly stated and supported; appropriately organized paragraphs or sections; logically sequenced (coherence); connectives appropriately used (cohesion)
	16–12	**Good to average:** Uneven expression, but main ideas stand out; paragraphing or section organization evident; logically sequenced (coherence); some connectives used (cohesion)
	11–8	**Fair to poor:** Very uneven expression, ideas difficult to follow; paragraphing/organization does not help the reader; logical sequence difficult to follow (coherence); connectives largely absent (cohesion)
	7–5	**Very poor:** Lacks fluent expression, ideas very difficult to follow, little sense of paragraphing/organization; no sense of logical sequence (coherence); connectives not used (cohesion)
	4–0	**Inadequate:** Fails to address this aspect of the task with any effectiveness

Vocabulary	20–17	**Excellent to very good:** Wide range of vocabulary; accurate word/idiom choice and usage; appropriate selection to match register
	16–12	**Good to average:** adequate range of vocabulary; occasional mistakes in word/idiom choice and usage; register not always appropriate
	11–8	**Fair to poor:** limited range of vocabulary; a noticeable number of mistakes in word/idiom choice and usage; register not always appropriate
	7–5	**Very poor:** no range of vocabulary; uncomfortably frequent mistakes in word/idiom choice and usage; no apparent sense of register
	4–0	**Inadequate:** Fails to addres this aspect of the task with any effectiveness
Language	30–24	**Excellent to very good:** Confident handling of appropriate structures, hardly any errors of agreement. tense, number, word order, articles, pronouns, prepositions; meaning never obscured
	23–18	**Good to average:** Acceptable grammar - but problems with more complex structures; mostly appropriate structures; some errors of agreement. tense, number, word order, articles, pronouns, prepositions; meaning sometimes obscured
	17–10	**Fair to poor:** Insufficient range of structures with control only shown in simple constructions; frequent errors of agreement. tense, number, word order, articles, pronouns, prepositions; meaning sometimes obscured
	9–6	**Very poor:** Major problems with structures - even simple ones; frequent errors of negation, agreement. tense, number word order/function, articles, pronouns, prepositions; meaning often obscured
	5–0	**Inadequate:** Fails to address this aspect of the task with any effectiveness
Mechanics	10–8	**Excellent to very good:** Demonstrates full command of spelling, punctuation, capitalisation, layout
	7–5	**Good to average:** Occasional errors in spelling, punctuation, capitalisation, layout
	4–2	**Fair to poor:** Frequent errors in spelling, punctuation, capitalisation, layout
	1–0	**Very poor:** Fails to address this aspect of the task with any effectiveness

 TASK 77

What do you see as the potential advantages and disadvantages of such an evaluation scale?

Although this scale may appear cumbersome on first sight, it soon becomes easy to use and brings many advantages. Among these are:

1 Learners know the basis on which their work is being assessed. The marking scale is a public document. Ideally each student will have a copy of it to refer to, or one can be posted on a classroom notice-board.

2 Excellence in one aspect of the task can be recognized and weaknesses in other areas can be indicated. This helps learners to see where they are doing well and where they have problems. As these scores would usually be accompanied by a short personal response to the actual message of the text, the students have a well-rounded understanding of the impact their texts have had on their reader.

3 The system is extremely flexible.
 – Individual teachers, or groups of teachers in a school, can develop their own band-scales. A regional or national education authority can devise commonly agreed band-scales to suit local or national needs.
 – Score weighting (the percentage of the total score allocated to a particular area) can be adjusted in the light of the needs of the learners at a particular stage of development, or for a particular task. For example, with a total of 100 points available (this makes the maths easier!), a teacher may decide that for one group he or she is working with it would be appropriate to allocate 50 per cent of the marks to 'organization', sharing out the other marks between the other categories as appropriate.
 – New categories such as 'integration of diagrams / tables / charts' or 'awareness of audience' can be added to cater for a particular type of writing.

▶ TASK 78

Consider the difference between using the method of evaluation described above and the approach you normally use. Would you need to modify the scheme for your own purposes? If possible, use it to evaluate some completed writing that your students have done and discuss their reactions to this sort of assessment.

11.6 Examiner

The discussion of evaluation leads directly into the issue of the role of teacher as examiner. It is beyond the scope of this book to go into great detail about the examining and marking of writing. However, it is worth reminding ourselves of some basic principles of testing and examining to see how the evaluative framework proposed above can also be relevant to the teacher who has to take on the role of examiner.

It is generally recognized that a test of a language skill should be at least:

– *Valid*, i.e. it tests what it is supposed to test!—in our case a learner's ability to express him or herself in writing, usually in a given context
– *Reliable*, i.e. it will produce marks that can be reproduced if another marker rates the same script
– *Practical*, i.e. it can be done in a reasonable length of time and at an acceptable cost.

Clearly, as examiners, teachers must decide on writing tasks which will conform to these criteria. As far as validity is concerned, students on a business correspondence course should write business correspondence; in a culture where students are expected to write essays, essays will be in the examination. In the area of reliability, problems can arise in ensuring a degree of agreement between markers as to what constitutes a 'good' answer and what constitutes an answer which will fail. And when it comes to the practicality of a test, teachers should bear in mind that written texts take longer to mark than, for example, multiple-choice questions. This has implications both for the length of the answers required, and the time available for marking them.

▶ TASK 79

Using the band-scale system described and illustrated above, how could you ensure that teachers marking examination scripts gave reliable and consistent grades?

The most common way of achieving 'inter-marker' reliability is to hold regular standardization meetings where teams of teachers work together to mark a set of scripts addressing the same task. In a large school, this might be a team of colleagues. In the case of smaller schools, teachers working in a town or region can join forces. Teachers can use a band scale to give both detailed and global marks to a script and then discuss the grades they have allocated. There may sometimes be quite wide divergence at the beginning of this operation, especially if teachers are unfamiliar with the marking scheme. However, this divergence soon disappears and most experienced teachers are able to establish a consensus on scoring in a two- or three-hour standardization session. Reliability has to be maintained by further short meetings, usually before each examination, and teams of senior examiners will also 'spot-check' samples of scripts to ensure the reliability of rating across a regional or national system.

The approach that has been outlined here can be applied to a single school or to an international examination system (it is the basic method used, for example, by the University of Cambridge Local Examinations Syndicate).

11.7 Conclusion

In 11 we have drawn together the main threads of our discussion of approaches to writing and the ways in which teachers can help learners write more effectively. We have seen how teachers—and, in the case of the first three roles, students—can be audience, assistant, evaluator, or examiner and how these roles can be taken on at different stages in a writing process. We have also seen how contrasting approaches to the teaching of writing will influence the kind of feedback that a teacher might wish to give and how the four types of knowledge that a writer needs in order to write successfully—knowledge of content, context, language system, and the writing process—can provide a framework for the comments that teachers make on drafts and completed texts.

As we said earlier, a text is never 'finished', it is simply that the writer has to stop writing at some point. We have now seen some of the ways in which teachers can help learners arrive at what they feel is a satisfactory final version of their text. The next task is to explore in more detail, and in a way which makes a direct connection with the classroom, some of the different ways in which teachers and learners can evaluate and use the ideas that have been presented in Section One and Section Two.

Exploration

12 Exploring writing in the classroom

As is clear from our previous discussion, the term 'writing' can be ambiguous. It can be an 'activity' which takes place in the classroom or elsewhere. It can also be a 'product', in the sense of the texts which writers produce. In this section, we shall inevitably find ourselves investigating both these aspects.

The tasks in this section have been designed to provide you with opportunities to relate the discussion in the first two sections to your own experience, and to help in the development of practical research activities that you can carry out either alone or with groups of colleagues. Many of the activities presented here involve teachers and students working together in the classroom. The tasks can be worked on in any order, but they are presented in a sequence which matches the development of the arguments in Sections One and Two.

▶ TASK 80

Aim
To find out about the needs of learners at the beginning of a writing course.

Resources
The discussion on Tasks 1, 2, and 4.
Multiple copies of a questionnaire.

Procedure
Prepare a questionnaire for use at the beginning of a writing course in an institution where you teach. An example has been given below, but the form of your questionnaire will depend on the priorities that you have in undertaking your investigation.

City College Writing Program Year one questionnaire				
Name		Class		
Main subject		Subsidiary subject		
I feel confident writing: agree 1 don't know 2 disagree 3	lecture notes short reports	exam essays long reports	seminar papers business letters	
I like to write:				
I hate writing:				
I use a wordprocessor for personal writing	all the time	sometimes	never	
I use a wordprocessor for study assignments	all the time	sometimes	never	
Please return this form to your course director before the first Friday of the semester We will use this information in planning our teaching program Thanks ...				

The questionnaire can be given to students when they register for a class, but before teaching begins, or can be completed as part of the first session of a writing course.

Evaluation

Learners in different groups can have very different interests and needs. Using questionnaires at the beginning of a writing course can give you information that will help you tailor your teaching programme to suit your students. In the case of the questionnaire given above, the teacher was able to use the data she obtained from two groups of eighteen students to plan a much greater emphasis on writing for examinations than she had originally intended. She found that these learners 'hated' writing exam essays, but this was largely because they lacked confidence in doing this sort of writing. In follow-up discussion of the questionnaire, the class agreed that it would be a good area on which to focus.

▶ TASK 81

Aim
To enable learners to understand the variety of starting points that students in the same group may have, and to help them see how previously-established language skills can be relevant in a foreign language writing class.

Resources
The discussion on Tasks 2 and 4.

Examples of writing provided by learners themselves. An optional evaluation sheet.

Procedure
1 Ask students to bring an example of their own writing that they feel pleased with to class. Explain that this can be a piece of personal writing or something that they have done for professional or study purposes. If you are teaching a monolingual group, it can be in the students' first language. If you are teaching a group from mixed language backgrounds, it should be written in the target language.

2 Students work in pairs or groups of three. Writers should say for whom their texts were written and why, and why they are satisfied with them.

3 Students read each other's texts and comment on the impact the writing has on them. It can be useful to have a report sheet such as the following to encourage positive comments.

```
This piece of writing is about:

Things I liked in this piece of writing are:
1
2

Things I found difficult to understand in this piece
(if any) are:
1
2

Other comments:
```

Evaluation
1 It is important for learners to get a sense of how to evaluate the quality of a piece of writing. Developing evaluation skills at an early point in the programme enables them to take a full part in peer-editing and conferencing activities as they are introduced into the course.

2 What aspects of a text might you want intermediate students to focus on? Would these be very different from the focus of a group of advanced learners?

▶ TASK 82

Aim
To help learners investigate the different roles of written language in their own language community or communities.

Resources
The discussion on Tasks 7 and 8.
Materials to make wall posters or OHP transparencies.

Procedure
1 Learners find out from three members of their family, or friends, about occasions on which they *have* to use writing. Ask them to think about religious and other cultural contexts as well as the more obvious administrative ones.

2 Learners report back in groups of four to six. Each group produces a wall poster or OHP transparency which summarizes their findings.

3 The class reads the posters and then works with the teacher to collate this information into a description of the functions of written language in their country (or countries if it is a multilingual class).

4 An account of the results of this survey can be given as a first writing assignment for the group.

Evaluation
Learners can benefit from having a clear understanding of how writing is used in their first language culture and the extent to which, if at all, this differs from its use in the foreign language culture. Such an understanding helps them to develop a sense of the relationship between writer and audience and to see how the purpose of a text determines the way a writer chooses organizational patterns, grammatical structures, and vocabulary.

▶ TASK 83

Aim
To provide learners with experience in adapting the style of a text so that it acquires a new purpose. To let learners draw on the insights that they have developed into the contrasts between conversational language use and more formal written texts.

Resources
The discussion in 3.1.

Examples of authentic spoken text. Transcripts of listening materials can sometimes be an excellent source of this sort of material. The example below comes from Harmer (1989).

Well, I think the good point about London is that London is still a very tolerant and very relaxed place, and most people, I find, are very friendly. It's still a very fluid society—if you go to America, you find a much more ghettoized society in terms of races, where you have middle-class blacks and middle-class white ghettos, whereas in this society you don't have that rigid, that rigid sort of ghettoized society, even in Brixton, which is supposed to be, you know, the black area in London you find, sort of middle-class white people and black people living side by side, it's still a much more mixed and heterogeneous society than, than America. And it is in many ways—in London—an open and a tolerant society.

(*Harmer: Listening File 1989*)

Procedure

1 In groups of three or four, learners discuss the context in which the spoken text was produced (in this case an informal interview) and identify the sorts of message that the text provides, i.e. both its factual content and the interpersonal messages that are signalled.

2 Each group agrees a summary of the factual content of the text and writes this up as a set of notes.

3 The group then agree on a suitable reader (or readership) for a written version of the text, for example the text above might be adapted to form an extract from a 'rough guide' to London.

4 Individually, learners draft a new text drawing on the original factual information, but now using an appropriate style for the new context.

5 In their group, learners review each other's drafts and ensure that each text is appropriate to the new context.

6 Learners exchange texts with other groups. They must now identify the new contexts that the other groups have established for their texts, and justify their decisions by referring to textual evidence.

Evaluation

Part of the pleasure of learning to write at a more advanced level is the discovery that a writer can have a range of voices. By working collaboratively and matching text to purpose, learners can gain confidence in playing with the language.

▶ ## TASK 84

Aim

To give learners an opportunity to become more aware of the ways in which formal written and informal conversational language can differ, and to make sure that learners share a basic language for talking *about* language.

Resources

The discussion on Tasks 12, 13, 14, 15, and 16.

You will need brief extracts from relatively formal written texts and also short transcripts of conversations in the foreign language, or similar materials in the learners' first language. As these texts only need to be short it is preferable to try to collect your own bank of authentic materials. Unscripted conversations from the BBC World Service or Voice of America can be a useful source of this sort of data for learners of English (but avoid scripted news broadcasts, documentaries, or interviews).

Procedure

1 Divide your class into three sets of groups of four to six students, and give them all copies of the same texts.

2 Ask one set of groups to focus on simple grammatical categories like 'verb' or 'noun' and to assess relative frequencies.

3 Ask another set of groups to focus on vocabulary and to assess which texts use more or less common vocabulary.

4 Ask the third set of groups to focus on clause length and complexity. (NB for students of English, useful sources of information about frequency and on spoken and written use are the *Longman Dictionary of Contemporary English*, and *Collins COBUILD Dictionary*).

5 Once information has been collected and discussed (the teacher is an important informant and consultant at this stage in the activity) the groups present their findings to the class. This information can be tabulated and used as the basis for future comparisons with texts that the learners write.

Evaluation

This activity works especially well when language awareness is seen as an important part of the overall language learning programme. Whether learners are working on foreign language texts or data taken from their first language, they gain an ability to identify and comment on important contrasts in language use, and develop confidence in dealing with the way in which they themselves use language as writers.

▶ ## TASK 85

Aim

To increase learners' awareness of the ways in which texts can be written in widely differing styles, and to begin an investigation of the impact of these stylistic choices on readers.

Resources

The discussion on Task 17.

A collection of written texts or text extracts of paragraph length taken from a variety of sources. Newspaper extracts (tabloid and quality) dealing with the same story can be a useful source of materials. You may want to reduce the number of clues about where the texts come from by retyping them or copying out short passages by hand. This activity can also be done on the board or OHP with the teacher presenting contrasting texts and working with students on the differences between them.)

Procedure

1 Divide students into groups of three or four and hand out copies of the extracts.

2 Explain that their task is to decide on the sources of the extracts (for example, quality newspaper, direct mail, textbook). They should also comment on the likely purpose and readership of each text.

3 Groups report back to the class. If there is disagreement between groups then this gives an opportunity for a discussion of the evidence that each group has used in coming to its conclusions.

Evaluation

At the beginning of a writing course, especially one moving towards advanced skills, it is important for learners to appreciate the very wide range of possible styles that are available to expert writers, and to be clear about the contexts in which each different style may be appropriate.

► **TASK 86**

Aim

To identify the way in which the organization of specific texts is determined by their social function.

Resources

The discussion on Tasks 18 and 19.

A selection of mail order catalogues, either in the foreign language or (in monolingual classes) in the learners' first language. Try and get hold of contrasting examples from both up-market companies and more mass-market companies. Alternatively, you could use holiday brochures.

Procedure

1 Ask your students, in groups of three or four, to discuss the types of information that a mail order company might want to communicate to its customers. Also, ask them to discuss the different sorts of information that potential customers in different market sectors may be looking for.

2 Give two or three examples of different catalogues to each group. Ask the students to identify the extent to which the writers of the catalogues have been successful in organizing the texts so that readers can find information quickly and efficiently.

3 The groups prepare a presentation of their findings and report back to the class.

4 Ask the students to comment on the ways in which they might use the ideas about text organization that have come out of this activity in their own writing.

Evaluation

This activity gives students a very practical insight into the importance of layout and consistency of organization in texts which are doing a specific job. They should be encouraged to consider the ways in which they can use layout in their own writing to make their texts 'user-friendly'. Inserting adequate space between paragraphs is a simple example of how to ease text processing.

▶ **TASK 87**

Aim

To heighten learner awareness of the predictability of text organization in much factual writing.

Resources

The discussion in Tasks 20 and 21.

Samples of texts with content that will be of interest to the learners. Short articles from popular magazines with some specialist interest (computers, fashion, sport, cars, music, etc.) work well. Retype the texts double-spaced, and then split them up into paragraphs. A word processor is useful in preparing materials for this activity.

Procedure

1 Divide the class into groups of three or four. Provide each group with one collection of jumbled paragraphs to reconstitute as a complete text. (Check that you can do this yourself before you give it to the students! If it is too difficult to do it paragraph by paragraph, then keep some paragraphs together.)

2 Once a group has agreed on a sequence, they must prepare a presentation for the class in which they explain their reasons for the organization of their sequence. They should be able to talk about the function of each element in the text and their reasons for agreeing on their chosen sequence (for example, SITUATION—PROBLEM—SOLUTION/RESPONSE—EVALUATION/RESULT; GENERAL—PARTICULAR; reference devices).

Evaluation

In this activity, learners are able to focus on the different systems which operate ensure the cohesion and coherence of written texts. A variation on this activity is for the teacher to reveal a paragraph statement by statement on the board or an OHP, and work with the class to reconstruct the 'dialogue with the reader' implicit in the text.

▶ TASK 88

Aim
To work with learners in investigating the variety of processes they make use of across a range of writing tasks.

Resources
The discussion on Tasks 26, 27, and 28.

Examples of texts and writing tasks that are relevant to your students, either in a context of a school syllabus or in their work or study.

Procedure
1 Prepare seven or eight examples of different texts, or tasks that would produce such texts. For example with a class preparing for a public language examination, these might include formal and informal letters, an essay, a list, a postcard, a telegram, a dialogue, a narrative, and a description.
2 Learners work in small groups to divide the texts or tasks into two or three sets: those which need a lot of planning, those which need less, and, if appropriate, those that need none at all.
3 Ask learners to prepare reasons for their decisions. These will cover issues such as the need for spontaneity in some sorts of writing, and the way a writer's previous experience of certain texts can reduce their need to prepare a formal plan.
4 Learners present their categorizations to other students and discuss the extent to which useful generalizations about writing processes can be made.

Evaluation
Learners need to be aware that there can be many different writing processes, each the result of the needs of different writers faced with different tasks. Such an awareness can be particularly helpful for learners preparing for examinations in which they will have to write essay answers. If they realize that an extensive plan is not appropriate for this sort of task, *but* that some planning can be very helpful, this can greatly assist them in performing a difficult and stressful task. Matching the amount of preparation to the task is a skill in its own right.

▶ TASK 89

Aim
To investigate contrasts between prototypical genres of writing, for example DESCRIPTION and REPORT (see **6.2**), and to show how changes in communicative purpose necessitate changes in the text.

Resources
The discussion on Task 34. Personal descriptions written by learners as part of the assignment in Stage 1.

Procedure

Stage 1

1 Learners write a description of an activity that has a personal dimension and which they enjoy (for example family festivals, games they play in their family or with friends, or they way they prepare a meal). The audience for this text is the teacher. The task could be part of a 'getting to know you' activity at an early point in a course.

2 The teacher agrees to write a similar description for the whole class to read.

3 Students are told that the texts will be used in another writing activity later in the course.

4 The descriptions are written, read and commented on. One copy of each description is kept by the teacher.

Stage 2

1 Students are introduced to report-writing. This introduction should include discussion of why reports are written, the sorts of audience they might have, and the aspects of language use associated with them (for example, organization, grammar, and vocabulary).

2 Learners are set the task of writing a report on, for example, the different roles that girls and boys / men and women take in domestic work, or the importance of public festivals in different students' lives. Explain that they will use a selection of the descriptions written in Stage 1 as data.

3 In groups of three or four, learners select a focus for their report and the descriptions that they will use as data. At this point, you could add some descriptions written by another class, but obtain the writers' permission first. The group plans their report and then individuals write draft sections. These are collated and then read and revised by the group to ensure that the style and format of the final report are appropriate to the task and internally consistent.

4 Reports are exchanged between groups and the differences between the original descriptions and the reports are discussed.

5 After any final adjustments are made, the reports are commented on by the teacher.

Evaluation

A long-term project of this kind helps create a community of readers and writers in the classroom, and gives learners important insights into the ways in which writing purpose affects the nature of texts. The table below indicates some of the prototypical genres that can be investigated in this way.

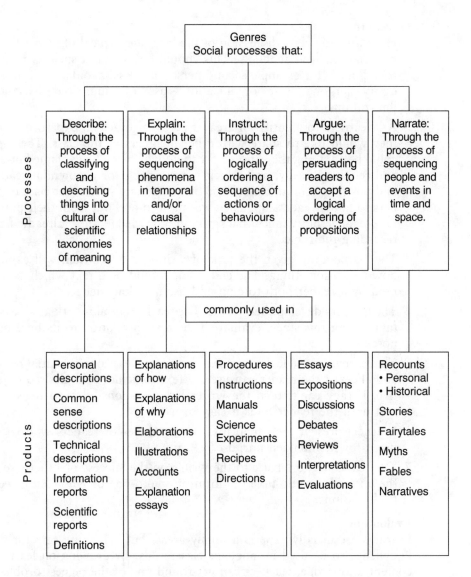

Genres
Social processes that:

| Describe: Through the process of classifying and describing things into cultural or scientific taxonomies of meaning | Explain: Through the process of sequencing phenomena in temporal and/or causal relationships | Instruct: Through the process of logically ordering a sequence of actions or behaviours | Argue: Through the process of persuading readers to accept a logical ordering of propositions | Narrate: Through the process of sequencing people and events in time and space. |

Processes

commonly used in

Personal descriptions	Explanations of how	Procedures	Essays	Recounts
Common sense descriptions	Explanations of why	Instructions	Expositions	• Personal • Historical
Technical descriptions	Elaborations	Manuals	Discussions	Stories
Information reports	Illustrations	Science Experiments	Debates	Fairytales
Scientific reports	Accounts	Recipes	Reviews	Myths
Definitions	Explanation essays	Directions	Interpretations	Fables
			Evaluations	Narratives

Products

(*Callaghan, Knapp, and Noble 1993:193*)

▶ TASK 90

Aim
To draw on the content knowledge that learners have developed through their personal, professional, or educational experience and use it in writing in an instructional genre.

Resources
The discussion in 6, and Tasks 37 and 38. Learners' own experience. This can be in other subjects in a school curriculum, or professional expertise, or an area of personal interest such as a sport or hobby.

Procedure

1 Have a whole-class discussion of the language typical of instructional materials such as manuals. This should cover issues such as reader-friendliness (for example second person address, avoidance of unnecessary jargon, clear organization, use of numbered lists and illustrations).

2 Ask learners to identify an area of personal practical expertise which they would like to share with other members of the class. The topic could be anything they know how to do which can be explained briefly and relatively easily, and which is interesting for a potential reader, and possible to do in class. They then negotiate with other class members to find a readership. They will need to find out from their potential readers how much background knowledge they already have regarding the topic.

3 The learners are given the task of writing a text which will explain how to do something. The end result should be a text which can be used by a reader both to gain and use new knowledge.

4 The learners develop their drafts. The teacher should work as an assistant during this stage, evaluating the text in relation to its final purpose.

5 The learners present their second draft to at least one potential reader and check if the reader can use the text to achieve the desired objective. If they can't, then the writer has a responsibility to revise the text until the reader finds it easy to use.

6 Learners present their final texts to a number of readers who try to use it for its intended purpose.

7 The readers report back to the writer on the success or otherwise of the text. This could take the form of one-to-one or whole-class feedback sessions.

Evaluation

Learners are usually experts in many areas, but it is quite rare for this knowledge to be used in language classrooms. By drawing on learners' content knowledge, teachers can get round one of the biggest problems that they face in writing classes. And learners usually enjoy assuming the role of expert or instructor.

▶ **TASK 91**

Aim

To give learners an opportunity to build their own text concordance without access to a computer, and in this way to increase their vocabulary in the target language.

Resources
The discussion on Task 39. A class of at least twelve students. For this activity, thirty or more learners is an advantage (the project could be undertaken by more than one class).

Access to an extensive collection of texts of a genre of interest to your students (examples might include sports journalism, record reviews, or specialist textbooks).

Procedure
1 Explain to the students that they will be investigating vocabulary and grammar in a specific genre of writing, and decide what this genre should be.

3 Ask learners to spend a limited time each week reading texts in the genre chosen, and to collect new or unusual uses of, for example, verb + preposition. They should use dictionaries or other sources of information to check their understanding of the expressions in context.

4 Ask learners are asked to write out the word or expression along with about five words of context to the left and the right of the first letter of the word. They should write the keyword in the middle of the line on a narrow slip of paper, as in the example below:

of our cities? First, it should be **held up** for critical inspection, pilloried whatever

5 At the end of each week, learners bring together the examples that have interested them and see if they have identified similar vocabulary.

6 The following set of examples was collected by students who were interested in the ways in which 'thing' could be used in English. They collected them from a variety of sources (mostly newspapers) during a week's reading.

```
 ve" institution - sex was a bad  thing  because it interfered with the
 e middle of our towns. The best  thing  would be to put a cap on the s
   they choose to work in, a good  thing. Modern British architects wor
 rs will be added. The important  thing  is that the Thirty Year Rule i
     This was obviously the last  thing  on their minds. With its shimm
 arate talents together, to make  things happen that otherwise might n
 us data to find out the sort of  thing  at least is certain: if Britis
   complement one another, is one  thing. Effecting change in an econom
 an, adolescent to say some pithy  things about divides both cultural a
       Perhaps the market will sort  things out after all. If the station
   loved does not care about such  things.   The attitudes towards archi
 Uchida explained it, 'the whole  thing  is an extreme representation o
```

7 Learners can investigate different aspects of how the word is used by alphabetically sorting the slips of paper according to the word immediately to the left or right of the 'key' word. The example above has been sorted by the word to the left of the key word.

Evaluation
Although computer concordances can give this sort of information more quickly, there can be advantages to manual data collection, the major one being that learners are more likely to remember words that they have compared and sorted in this way.

▶ **TASK 92**

Aim
To demonstrate the difference between prototypical genres and specialist genres.

Resources
The discussion in 7. Specialist texts from as wide a range of different genres as you can find, for example 'academic' (laboratory notes, journal articles, school reports); 'legal' (wills, guarantees, contracts); 'financial' (life insurance documents, bank statements, share certificates); 'journalistic' (law reports, sports writing, editorial comment). Ideally you will need at least three examples of each genre chosen.

Procedure
1 Give a selection of texts from a variety of genres to each group of three or four students and ask them to sort these into different categories. If possible, students should assign a genre name to the category to which each text belongs.

2 When they have sorted their texts into genre categories, learners should choose one genre to study. Give them as many example texts as possible from the genre they have chosen.

3 Ask students to prepare a description of the essential features of their chosen genre. Tell them to organize it under headings such as:
   – communicative purpose of the text
   – expected audience(s)
   – relative authority of the writer in the interaction
   – key organizational features
   – key grammatical features
   – key vocabulary features.

Evaluation
By working with real-world examples of texts and seeing how their organization and wording contribute to their effectiveness in specific contexts, learners develop an awareness of the relationship between the social function of a text and the choices a writer makes about its organization, grammar, and vocabulary.

If learners have a particular interest in a single genre, this activity can be used, but omitting the element of choice at the beginning. As an extension to stage 3, students can be asked to identify texts that are most prototypically representative of current writing in the genre being studied.

▶ TASK 93

Aim
To give learners the opportunity of writing for real audiences and to experiment with different genres of writing.

Resources
Access to other learners, ideally in different classes.

Procedure
1 Working in groups of three or four, learners decide which audience they will be writing for. This might be other individuals in their class, but it is more interesting if the audience is students in other classes, or even other years. This could mean senior students writing for junior students, or students writing for a group with specific interests or needs.
2 Learners decide on the content and text-type that will be of interest for their projected readers. For example this could be a school guide for visiting exchange students, or a simplified reader for junior classes.
3 They then work together to produce suitable written material.
4 Learners present their materials to their audience. In the examples above, this could be in a 'welcome' talk referring to the guide, or a live reading of stories written for junior classes.

Evaluation
An excellent project of this sort has been done around reading material based on large-page books for young learners ('big books'). In this project learners were given training in how to use the big books in group reading activities, and went into junior classes as 'teaching assistants'. Their sense of satisfaction in being able to write stories that genuinely engaged younger learners' interest was considerable, and the reading materials are still being used in the school's resource bank. By putting student writing to real use, teachers have the benefit of getting additional teaching materials to use with other classes, and learners have the satisfaction of seeing their writing being enjoyed by readers.

▶ TASK 94

Aim
To give learners the opportunity to identify the techniques for generating

ideas and for planning (for example mind-maps, brainstorming, listing, structured outlining) that are most appropriate to their own learning style.

Resources
The activities in Tasks 61, 62, and 63. It is also helpful to have examples of plans and the results of ideas-generating activities carried out by other groups of learners.

Procedure
1 Present a range of ideas-generating and planning techniques to learners. This can be done over a period of weeks or during a single lesson. This presentation should combine a description of a technique with an opportunity to review the ways in which other learners have used it.

2 Agree on a writing task with the class. It is usually best if this task has a commonly agreed purpose, although students can be offered a choice of theme. Activities such as reviews of consumer goods (for example convenience foods) are one possibility.

3 Ask learners to select one or two of the ideas-generating and planning techniques you have presented and to use them as they prepare to write.

4 After the writing task has been completed, ask learners to report on the techniques they used and to comment on how they felt about using them. Ask them to consider what techniques they might find useful for a different kind of writing task, for example a piece of imaginative writing rather than a factual report.

Evaluation
Learners can identify which planning techniques they feel most comfortable with, and can also see how some techniques might be more useful in some contexts than others. They also gain a practical awareness of the value that ideas-generating and planning can have in their own practice as writers.

▶ TASK 95

Aim
This is a variation on Task 94. Its main purpose is to review different approaches to pre-writing activities taken by students in a class. It is best done after learners have been given an introduction to the use of plans in factual writing tasks.

Resources
The discussion on Tasks 61, 62, and 63. An agreed writing task (for example a persuasive report, a description of a process, explanatory instructions). Examples of plans prepared by students in the same class.

Procedure

1 Students agree on a writing task.

2 In groups of three or four, they discuss issues raised by the task and agree on readership and focus. (This can involve ideas-generating activities like mind-mapping, brainstorming, and listing.)

3 Individually learners prepare initial plans of what they intend to write, using whatever approach they feel comfortable with.

4 In their groups, learners compare plans and decide if they want to draw on ideas or perspectives provided by other group members.

5 Learners amend their plans in the light of this discussion and write their tasks.

Evaluation

This task, and the one which follows, give learners an opportunity to reflect on different ways of planning writing tasks, and also demonstrate the benefits of sharing ideas with other students during the planning process.

▶ **TASK 96**

Aim

This task follows on from Task 95. It aims to show learners how a plan is only a starting point for a text, and that it is common for writers to abandon parts of their original plan as they develop a text.

Resources

The initial plans prepared by learners in Task 95. The final texts written by learners following Task 95 (after drafting, revision, and editing).

Procedure

1 Learners work in pairs. Each student explains their writing plan to their partner and then learners read each other's texts, noting any variations in organization, content, or focus from the original plan.

2 Learners discuss the variations between the plan and the final text, and the writer's reasons for making changes.

3 Whole-class discussion of learners' experience of working with plans can follow.

Evaluation

It is important for learners to realize that a plan is only a starting point and that texts often change in quite fundamental ways as they are developed. This activity helps learners see how texts relate to plans, but rarely follow them exactly.

▶   TASK 97

Aim
To investigate the advantages and disadvantages of using different marking codes when responding to learners' writing.

Resources
The discussion in **11**, especially Tasks 71 and 77.

Procedure
1 Introduce learners to a marking code such as the one given below, and explain that you will be using this during the coming weeks of the course.

spelling error	*Sp*
word order error	*WO (◠)*
verb form error	*V*
tense error	*T*
article error	*Art*
preposition error	*Pp*
wrong word	*WW*
missing word	*∧*
subject / verb concord error	*SV*
sentence structure error	*SS*

2 Decide how you will use the code, for example underlining problems in the text and putting the code immediately above; putting the code in the margin and underlining the error, or putting the code in the margin but leaving the exact location of the error unmarked. If you choose to focus on specific language problems, tell the students which ones you plan to deal with, for example use of articles, sentence structure, or tense.

3 Once you have returned the marked work to your students, discuss the way you have used the codes with them. By experimenting over a period of weeks you will find out which way of marking is most suited to different writing activities, and will have involved your students in establishing an agreed system for giving feedback on their work.

Evaluation
By assessing feedback techniques with learners, it is possible to gain their involvement in the process of text improvement, and to identify what sort of information they feel they need are likely to use.

▶ TASK 98

Aim
To evaluate different approaches to giving feedback on writing and what to focus on in relation to particular types of writing activity.

Resources
The discussion in **11**. A group of learners whom you are teaching for more than one term or semester. A series of agreed writing activities relevant to the needs of the learners.

Procedure
1 Explain to the learners that you are going to be experimenting with different ways of giving feedback during the course.

2 Over a period of weeks, use different approaches to giving feedback and discuss the advantages and disadvantages of each of them with the learners.

3 After, for example, a term, agree with the class on the approaches to giving feedback that seem most appropriate for particular types of writing activity. Apply these consistently throughout the rest of the year. These procedures can be reviewed at the end of the year and further adjustments made.

Evaluation
By involving learners more in the process of giving and receiving feedback, the teacher can help them to take greater responsibility for the quality of their own writing. As they become more aware of what differentiates a successful from an unsuccessful text, they are able to hand in much better final texts, thereby reducing the marking load for the teacher!

▶ TASK 99

Aim
To help learners identify the sorts of errors that they are making by letting them share the experience of other students in the group.

Resources
Examples of writing done by students in the same learning group.

Procedure
1 While preparing evaluations of final drafts, collect any errors that it might be useful for the whole class to focus on.

2 Write out the sentences containing these mistakes on the board or an OHP transparency.

3 Ask learners to identify the mistake, and suggest corrections or improvements. An example of a set of such 'problems' is given below. In this case a group of European student teachers had written reports on statistics indicating changes in smoking habits.

> —— Figures on smoking recently issued by Health Department officials clearly demonstrate the correlation of smokers among different social groups.
> —— Figures on smoking recently issued by Health Department officials clearly demonstrate the role of education in observing a healthy way of life.
> —— First there is a general tendency with educated versus non-educated workers in the UK.
> —— Figures on smoking recently issued by Health Department officials clearly demonstrates that there exists a connection between the amount of smokers and their belonging to a particular social group.
> —— And finally there are professionals who do not stand well with cigars and cigarettes, as only 15 percent persue smoking.

Evaluation
By working on collections of mistakes like this, learners become more aware of the persistent problems that they have when writing in the foreign language, and are better able to recognize other learners' mistakes, and their own.

Glossary

bottom up: a way of processing information or solving a problem which makes use of data that is already available in order to arrive at new knowledge; see also **schema**.

clause: a group of words which form a grammatical unit and which contain a subject and a finite verb.

clause complex: a group of clauses combined in a single grammatical unit. It is sometimes a more useful term than 'sentence' as it can be used as a unit of description for both written and spoken language.

coherence: the relationships which link the meanings of utterances in a spoken text or the sentences in a written text. These can be established by the use of logical or sequence connectors (for example, *therefore, next*), or can result from the writer's use of common ways of organizing meanings in texts, for example patterns such as GENERAL —PARTICULAR; SITUATION/PROBLEM—SOLUTION—EVALUTION/ RESULT.

coherent: the quality a text has when the meanings of utterances or sentences are clearly related to one another in a logical sequence; see also **coherence**.

cohesion: the grammatical and lexical relationships between the different elements of a text. These can include the direct types of relationships which exist between subjects and verbs, or the less direct relationships between, for example pronouns and the words or phrases to which they refer.

cohesive: the quality a text has as the result of the correct use of the grammatical and lexical relationships between its different elements; see also **cohesion**.

commitment: a way of describing the extent to which a writer has been willing to take responsibnility for the truth and authority of the assertions he or she is making; see also **hedging**.

communicative event: a moment of communication which can easily be distinguished from other moments. For example a job interview is a spoken communicative event. A piece of writing can form part of a single communicative event, for example a love letter, or it can be involved in many communicative events. For example an advertisement may be read by millions of people, producing millions of separate events each time the text is read and responded to.

communicative purpose: the results that the writer hopes to achieve in writing a text. This may be a general purpose such as 'to entertain', or may be very specific, for example 'to make sure that X amount of money is transferred from my bank account to a service provider's bank account by a particular date'.

competence: in the context of writing, competence refers not only to the ability of a writer to apply the grammatical rules of a language in order to form grammatically correct sentences, but also to the writer's ability to select appropriate grammar and vocabulary in order to achieve their **communicative purpose**.

composing: a stage in the process of writing a complete text. During composition, a writer draws on preparatory reading or other research, but may also discover a need to do further research before the text can be completed.

concordance: a sampling of text in which a specific word or phrase is printed in the context in which it appears, with a given number of characters to the right and left of it.

content knowledge: the writer's understanding of the subject matter of his or her text. Without some form of content knowledge, a writer has no meaning to express. It is possible to write language learning exercises without content knowledge, but if a writer is to make a meaningful text he or she must have some form of content knowledge, even if this content is entirely imaginary.

context knowledge: a writer's context knowlege makes is possible for him or her to write appropriate texts for particular readers. Context knowledge helps the writer to activate their **language system knowledge** and to select appropriate organizational patterns and appropriate wordings for a particular purpose. For example, if you have never seen a bibliography prepared to the APA standard, and are not given a set of guidance notes on how to prepare such a bibliography, you will not have enough context knowledge to complete this task satisfactorily.

corpus (plural **corpora**): a collection of texts that have been put together for a particular purpose. Nowadays, corpora are usually stored in an electronic format which can be studied with the assistance of a computer. A corpus can be very large (hundreds of millions of words), as is commonly the case with corpora that have been developed for dictionary making, or it can be highly specialized and quite small (tens of thousands of words).

description: in the context of genre studies, a personal account of factual or imagined events and phenomena. Because it does not attempt to be objective, it is largely unchallengeable; see **report**.

discourse: language that has been produced as a result of an act of communication.

discourse community: in the context of genre studies, a group of speakers or writers who share a communicative purpose, or set of communicative purposes, and use commonly agreed texts to achieve these purposes. For example a discourse community could be a widely scattered group of cigarette card collectors who share information through a newsletter which makes use of specialist terms and abbreviations, or it could be a university which requires Ph.D candidates to submit their theses in accordance with a set of agreed rules and standards.

discourse relations: larger structures in a text which are not directly expressed by the sequence of sentences, and which support the overall coherence of the text.

editing: the final stage in the writing process. During editing, writers try to correct surface problems in their texts, for example mistakes in spelling and grammar.

evaluation: in writing instruction, evaluation is often carried out by teachers, but it should be remembered that it can also be done by learners. Effective evaluation should provide two kinds of information to the writer: (1) Is the content relevant to the task and is it clearly expressed? (2) Does the writer use language accurately and appropriately?, and, in the case of writing part of whose purpose is to entertain: (3) Is the text interesting?

formality: in writing, the quality of a text which determines the sort of relationship which the writer wishes to establish with the reader. In English it is often associated with grammatical forms which are impersonal and which create maximum distance between the reader and the writer.

genre: a genre is a **communicative event** which uses texts in predictable ways to achieve agreed **communicative purposes.** LETTER is not a genre, but LETTER OF APPOINTMENT is as examples are likely to contain many predictable elements that are associated with this particular social action.

hedging: a process in which a writer reduces their commitment to a particular idea or opinion through, typically, the use of lexical or grammatical devices, for example 'I think that this idea may not be 100 per cent correct, but I could be wrong'; see **commitment.**

intellectual/rhetorical approach: an approach to teaching academic writing which assumes a common intellectual framework for all academic discourse. In this tradition the modes of classical rhetoric are taken as the starting point for instruction, and it is assumed that students have a primary need to gain a mastery of these rhetorical modes if they are to become competent writers in their chosen disciplines; see also **social/genre approach.**

language system knowledge: the ability to make appropriate grammatical and lexical choices when writing for a particular **communicative purpose.** In order to produce fully appropriate texts, writers also need **context knowledge.**

layout: the physical organization of a words, pictures, and other typographic devices on the page. In most societies certain kinds of texts have highly conventional layouts, for example funeral announcements, dictionaries, and business letters. The layout of other kinds of text, for example modern poetry, is less predictable.

lexis: the vocabulary of a language in contrast to its grammar.

lexical density: the ratio of the number of words to the number of clauses in a text. Written texts are more likely to have a high lexical density than spoken ones.

marked: see **unmarked**.

metalanguage: the language used for describing or analysing a language.

mind map: a way of representing associations between ideas graphically. It is used in some forms of note making and is a common device in planning writing or spoken presentations. It is sometimes called a 'spidergram' because it can show how centrally important ideas are connected to one other and to subsidiary ideas in a web-like network.

paralinguistic features: non-systematic aspects of language which can add meaning to what we say. They include the timbre of someone's voice (whether they are speaking loudly or softly, shouting or whispering), and the facial and other physical gestures they use when they speak.

process approach: an approach to the teaching of writing which stresses the creativity of the individual writer, and which pays attention to the development of good writing practices rather than the imitation of models.

process knowledge: the kind of knowledge which makes it possible for a writer to decide on the best way of going about a particular writing task. Process knowledge is the fourth kind of knowledge that a writer needs and complements **content, context,** and **language system** knowledge.

process writing: a way of describing the teaching methods associated with the **process approach**.

procedure: in the context of genre studies, a piece of writing about processes taking place in the world around you. Procedures attempt to generalize experience; see also **recount**.

prosodic features: the non-verbal aspects of spoken English that are used systematically to help give meaning to utterances: rhythm, phrasing, and pauses are among the most important of these.

protocol: in the context of writing research, a person's own account of his or her thoughts and ideas while doing a writing task.

recount: in the context of genre studies, a piece of writing which talks about a sequence of events from a personal point of view. The writer has no obligation to be factual or accurate, or to generalize from the experience being described; see also **procedure**.

report: in the context of genre studies, an impersonal accounts of facts; see also **description**.

schema (plural schemata): a generally accepted way of organizing ideas which provides a basis for readers' expectations of how a text will develop.

social/genre approach: an approach to teaching academic writing which focuses on the relationships between readers and writers in specific **discourse communities,** and on the texts that are used in creating or maintaining these relationships; see also **intellectual/rhetorical approach**.

style: the way a writer constructs a relationship with a possible reader. For example, a writer can adopt an intimate, highly personal style, or use a distant, impersonal style, depending on the relationship they wish to develop.

text: a piece of spoken or written language.

top-down: A top-down approach makes use of already established knowledge, expectations or understanding in order to solve a problem; see also **schema**.

unmarked: in English, sentences with the order Subject—Verb—Object (e.g. 'I like these people') are considered to be unmarked. But a sentence with the order Object—Subject—Verb (e.g. 'These people I like') is a **marked** form—it is possible, but unusual.

usage: refers to the way a linguistic item functions as an element in a linguistic system, for example the study of the passive as a part of the grammatical system of English, i.e. paying attention to how it is formed with auxiliary *be*; cf. **use**.

use: refers to the way a linguistic item functions as part of a system of communication, for example the study of the passive as part of a system which creates effects of formality, distance, and impersonality in English; cf **usage**.

writing process: the means whereby a text is produced. It includes all of the preparatory work a writer does before beginning writing, as well as the work that he or she does while writing and during revising and **editing**. It is now generally accepted that most writing processes are cyclical and non-linear rather than simple and linear.

Further Reading

Bhatia, V.K. 1993. *Analysing Genre: Language Use in Professional Settings*. Harlow: Longman.

A summary of the background to genre approaches to the study of written language, and a useful account of the application of these approaches in the teaching of English in legal and business contexts.

Halliday, M.A.K. 1989. *Spoken and Written Language*. Oxford: Oxford University Press.

An accessible linguistic account of the differences between spoken and written language. Using examples from English, Halliday shows how written and spoken language have developed in different ways in order to fulfil contrasting social functions.

Hedge, T. 1988. *Writing*. Oxford: Oxford University Press.

A practical guide to techniques in teaching writing. This book is especially useful in its treatment of process approaches to writing.

Kroll, B. 1990. *Second Language Learning: Research Insights for the Classroom*. Cambridge: Cambridge University Press.

This collection of essays provides a broad review of research in second language writing, drawing mainly on North American examples. The collection is useful for teachers who are considering doing their own research into teaching writing.

Martin, J. R. 1989. *Factual Writing: Exploring and Challenging Social Reality*. Oxford: Oxford University Press.

Martin focuses on writing in the school system, and argues for the inclusion of a much wider range of genres in the school writing syllabus. Although this book takes young children's writing as a starting point, it provides food for thought for all teachers of writing.

Swales, J. 1990. *Genre Analysis*. Cambridge: Cambridge University Press.

This book provides an account of the background to genre studies in the teaching of written language, and gives a framework for the use of genre approaches in the teaching of writing for academic purposes.

White, R., and **V. Arndt**. 1991. *Process Writing*. Harlow: Longman.

An excellent resource book for teachers who want practical ideas for helping students to get the most out of a writing course. Strongly humanistic in its approach, it draws on both American and British research.

Bibliography

Allwright, R.L., M-P. Woodley, and J.M. Allwright. 1988. 'Investigating reformulation as a practical strategy for the teaching of academic writing.' *Applied Linguistics* 9/3:237–58.

Andrews, R. G. H. 1990. *Written English for Business 2.* Oxford: Oxford University Press.

Arnold, J. and **J. Harmer.** 1978. *Advanced Writing Skills.* London: Longman.

Aronowitz, S. and **H. Giroux.** 1991. *Postmodern Education: Politics, Culture and Social Criticism.* Minneapolis, MN: University of Minnesota Press.

Bamforth, R. 1993. 'Process vs. genre: anatomy of a false dichotomy.' *Prospect* 8/1-2: 89–99.

Bartram, M. and **R. Walton.** 1991. *Mistake Management: A Positive Approach for Language Teachers.* Hove: Language Teaching Publications.

Bhatia, V. K. 1993. *Analysing Genre: Language Use in Professional Settings.* Harlow: Longman.

Bloor, T. and **J. Norrish.** (eds.). 1987. *Written Language.* Papers from the Annual Meeting of the British Association for Applied Linguistics. London: CILT/BAAL.

Bornat, R. 1987. *Programming from First Principles.* London: Prentice Hall.

Brindley, G. 1994. *Teaching English.* London: Routledge.

Brown, K. and **S. Hood.** 1989. *Writing Matters.* Cambridge: Cambridge University Press.

Bygate, M. 1987. *Speaking.* Oxford: Oxford University Press.

Byrne, D. 1988. *Teaching Writing Skills.* Harlow: Longman.

Callaghan, M., P. Knapp, and **G. Noble.** 1993. 'Genre in practice' in B. Cope and M. Kalantzis (eds.): *The Powers of Literacy: A Genre Approach to Teaching Writing.* London: Falmer Press.

Carrell, P., J. Devine, and **D. Eskey** (eds.). 1983. *Interactive Approaches to Second Language Reading.* Cambridge: Cambridge University Press.

Carrier, M. 1991. *Intermediate Language Skills. Writing.* Walton-on-Thames: Nelson.

Carroll, B. and **R. West** 1989. *The ESU Framework.* Harlow: Longman.

Cohen, A. D. 1983. 'Reformulating compositions'. *TESOL Newsletter* XVII/6:1–5.

Collins COBUILD English Dictionary. 1995 (new edition). London: Collins.

Cook, G. 1989. *Discourse.* Oxford: Oxford University Press.

Dewey, J. 1900a. *The School and Society.* Chicago: University of Chicago Press. (Reprinted in 1956).

Dewey, J. 1900b. *The Child and the Curriculum.* Chicago: University of Chicago Press. (Reprinted in 1956).

Doherty, M., L. Knapp, and S. Swift. 1987. *Write for Business.* Harlow: Longman.

Elliot, R. 1979. *The Bean Book.* London: Fontana/Collins.

Ellsworth, E. 1989. "Why doesn't this feel empowering? Working through the repressive myths of critical pedagogy.' *Harvard Education Review* 59/3: 297–324.

Fabb, N., D. Attridge, A. Durant, and C. MacCabe. 1987. *The Linguistics of Writing.* Manchester: University of Manchester Press.

Faigley, L. 1986. 'Competing theories of process: a critique and a proposal.' *College English* 48/6:527–42.

Fairclough, N. 1989. *Language and Power.* Harlow: Longman.

Færch, C. and G. Kasper. 1983. *Strategies in Interlanguage Communication.* Harlow: Longman.

Florio-Ruane, S. and S. Dunn. 1985. 'Teaching writing: some perennial questions and possible answers.' Occasional Paper No. 85, Michigan State University.

Flower, L. 1985. (second edition). *Problem-solving Strategies for Writing.* San Diego: Harcourt Brace Jovanovich.

Flower, L. and J. R. Hayes. 1977. 'Problem solving strategies and the writing process.' *College English* 39:449–61.

Flowerdew, J. 1993. 'An educational or process approach to the teaching of professional genres.' *ELT Journal* 47/4: 305–316.

Foggin, J. 1992. *Real Writing.* London: Hodder and Stoughton.

Foster, L. and M. Rado. 1993. 'The drive for literacy: are NESB women winners or losers?' *Prospect* 8/1–2:38–60.

Freedman, A., I. Pringle, and J. Yalden. 1983. *Learning to Write: First Language/Second Language.* Harlow: Longman.

Grigson, J. 1978. *Good Things.* Harmondsworth: Penguin.

Halliday, M. A. K. 1989. *Spoken and Written Language.* Oxford: Oxford University Press.

Halliday, M. A. K. and R. Hasan. 1985. *Language, Context and Text: Aspects of Language in a Social-Semiotic Perspective.* Oxford: Oxford University Press.

Halliday, M. A. K. and R. Hasan. 1976. *Cohesion in English.* Harlow: Longman.

Hamp-Lyons, L. and B. Heasley. 1987. *Study Writing.* Cambridge: Cambridge University Press.

Harmer, J. 1983. *The Practice of English Language Teaching.* Harlow: Longman.

Harmer, J. 1989. *The Listening File.* Harlow: Longman.

Harris, J. 1993. *Introducing Writing*. London: Penguin.

Harris, V. 1992. *The Cooking of Tuscany*. Cambridge: Martin Books (Simon and Schuster Consumer Books).

Hayes, J. R. and L. Flower. 1983. 'Uncovering cognitive processes in writing: an introduction to protocol analysis' in P. Mosenthal, L. Tamar, and S. A. Walmsley (eds.). *Research in Writing*. New York: Longman.

Hedge, T. 1988. *Writing*. Oxford: Oxford University Press.

Hilton, C. and M. Hyder. 1992. *Writing*. London: Letts Educational Ltd.

HMSO (1989). *English in the National Curriculum*. London: HMSO.

Hoey, M. (ed.) 1993. *Data, Description, Discourse*. London: HarperCollins.

Hoey, M. 1983. *On the Surface of Discourse*. London: George Allen and Unwin.

Hopkins, A. and C. Tribble. 1989. *Outlines*. Harlow: Longman.

Hopkins, A. 1989. *Perspectives*. Harlow: Longman.

Johns, A. M. 1988a. 'The discourse communities dilemma: identifying transferable skills for the academic milieu.' *English for Specific Purposes* 7/1:55–9.

Johns, A. M. 1988b. 'ESP and the future' in M. L. Tickoo (ed.) *ESP: State of the Art*. Singapore: RELC.

Jones, L. and R. Alexander. 1989. *International Business English*. Cambridge: Cambridge University Press.

Jordan, R. R. 1992. *Academic Writing Course*. London: Nelson.

Just, M. A. and P. A. Carpenter. 1977. *Cognitive Processes in Comprehension*. Hillsdale, NJ: Lawrence Erlbaum.

Krashen, S. 1984. *Writing Research: Theory and Applications*. Oxford: Pergamon.

Kress, G. 1982. *Learning to Write*. London: Routledge and Kegan Paul.

Kress, G. 1989. *Linguistic Processes in Sociocultural Practice*. Oxford: Oxford University Press.

Kress, G. 1994. *Learning to Write*. London: Routledge.

Kroll, B. 1990. *Second Language Learning: Research Insights for the Classroom*. Cambridge: Cambridge University Press.

Langan, J. 1993. *College Writing Skills with Readings*. New York: McGraw-Hill.

Lassalle, G. 1976. *The Adventurous Fish Cook*. London: Macmillan.

Leech, G. N. 1983. *Principles of Pragmatics*. Harlow: Longman.

Littlejohn, A. 1994. *Company to Company*. Cambridge: Cambridge University Press.

Magee, B. 1973. *Popper*. London: Fontana.

Martin, J. R. 1989. *Factual Writing: Exploring and Challenging Social Reality*. Oxford: Oxford University Press.

McDevitt, D. 1995. 'Recipe for disaster.' *Modern English Teacher* 4/2:41–5.

Millom, J. C. and **K. Tong** (eds.). 1991. *Text Analysis in Computer Assisted Language Learning*. Hong Kong: Hong Kong University of Science and Technology and City Polytechnic of Hong Kong.

Mohan, B. A. 1986. *Language and Content*. Reading, MA: Addison-Wesley.

Nystrand, M. 1987. *The Structure of Written Communication*. Orlando, FL: Academic Press Inc.

Owen, R. 1992. *BBC Business English*. London: BBC English.

Oxford Advanced Learners' Dictionary. 1995 (fifth edition). Oxford: Oxford University Press.

Perera, G. and **J. L. M. Trim** (eds.). 1971. *Applications of Linguistics*. Cambridge: Cambridge University Press.

Peters, P. (ed.). 1989. *The Macquarie Student Writer's Guide*. Milton: Jacaranda Press.

Protherough, R. and **J. Atkinson**. 1994. 'Shaping the image of the English teacher' in Brindley 1994.

Raimes, A. 1983. *Techniques in Teaching Writing*. New York: Oxford University Press.

Raimes, A. 1985. 'What unskilled ESL writers do as they write: a classroom study of composing'. TESOL Quarterly 19/2:229–58.

Raimes, A. 1993. 'Out of the woods: emerging traditions in the teaching of writing' in Silberstein 1993.

Richards, J., J. Platt, and **H. Weber**. 1985. *Longman Dictionary of Applied Linguistics*. Harlow: Longman.

Robinson, P. (ed). 1988. *Academic Writing: Process and Product*. Modern English Publications and The British Council.

Roden, C. 1985. *A New Book of Middle Eastern Food*. Harmondsworth: Penguin.

Sanford, A. J. and **S. C. Garrod**. 1981. *Understanding Written Language*. Chichester: Wiley.

Saulnier, L. 1914. *Le Répertoire de la Cuisine*. Staines: Jaeggi.

Silberstein, S . (ed.) 1993. *State of the Art TESOL Essays*. Alexandria, Va.: TESOL.

Sinclair, J. (ed). 1987. *Looking Up: An Account of the COBUILD Project in Lexical Computing*. London: Collins.

Sinclair, J. 1991. *Corpus, Concordance, Collocation*. Oxford: Oxford University Press.

Sommers, N. 1992. 'Between the drafts.' *College Composition and Communication* 43: 23–31.

Stubbs, M. 1987. 'An educational theory of (written) language' in Bloor and Norrish 1987.

Swales, J. 1990. *Genre Analysis*. Cambridge: Cambridge University Press.

Swan, M. and **C. Walter**. 1990 *New Cambridge English Course*. Cambridge: Cambridge University Press.

Tribble, C. 1991. 'Some uses of electronic text in English for academic purposes' in Millom and Tong 1991.

Tribble, C. and G. Jones. 1990. *Concordancing in the Classroom.* Harlow: Longman.

Tribble, C. 1990. 'Reformulation in a General English setting.' Occasional Papers, Bell Educational Trust.

Tribble, C. 1989. *Word for Word.* Harlow: Longman.

Turk, C. and J.Kirkman. 1989. *Effective Writing: Improving Scientific, Technical and Business Communication.* London: E. and F. N. Spon (Chapman and Hall).

Ure, J. 1971. 'Lexical density and register differentiation' in Perera and Trim 1971.

Wallace, C. 1992. *Reading.* Oxford: Oxford University Press.

White, R. and D. McGovern. 1994. *Writing.* Hemel Hempstead: Prentice Hall.

White, R. and V. Arndt. 1991. *Process Writing.* Harlow: Longman.

White, R. 1987. *Writing.* Oxford: Oxford University Press.

Widdowson, H. G. 1984. *Explorations in Applied Linguistics 2.* Oxford: Oxford University Press.

Willis, J. and D. Willis. 1988. *COBUILD English Course.* London: Collins.

Wilson, M. 1987. *Writing for Business.* Walton-on-Thames: Nelson.

Winter, E. O. 1976. 'Fundamentals of information structure'. Mimeo. Hatfield Polytechnic.

Winter, E. O. 1977. 'A clause relational approach to English texts: a study of some predicitve lexical items in written discourse'. *Instructional Science* 6/1: 1–92.

Zamel, V. 1983. 'The composing processes of advanced ESL students: six case studies.' *TESOL Quarterly* 17/2:165–87.

Zamel, V. 1985. 'Responding to student writing.' *TESOL Quarterly* 16/2:79–101

Zamel, V. 1993. 'Questioning academic discourse.' *College ESL* 3/1: 28–39.

Index

Entries relate to Section One, Two, and Three of the text, and to the glossary. References to the glossary are indicated by 'g' after the page number.

Acknowledgements

The author and publisher are grateful to the following for their kind permission to reproduce extracts and figures from copyright material:

BBC English for an extract from BBC *Business English* (1992) by R. Owen.

Cambridge University Press and the authors for extracts and figures from *Writing Matters* (1989) by K. Brown and S. Hood, *Study Writing* (1987) by L. Hamp-Lyons and B. Heasley, *New International Business English* (1996) by L. Jones and R. Alexander, *Company to Company* (1994) by A. Littlejohn, *Genre Analysis* (1990) by J. Swales, and *New Cambridge English Course* (1990) by M. Swan and C. Walter.

Chapman & Hall, International Thomson Publishing Services for extracts from *Effective Writing: Improving Scientific, Technical and Business Communications* (2e, 1989) by C. Turk and J. Kirkman.

COBUILD Ltd. for extracts from *The COBUILD English Language Dictionary* (Collins, 1987) and from *COBUILD English Course* (Collins, 1988) by J. and D. Willis.

Curtis Brown and HarperCollins Publishers for an extract from *The Bean Book* (Fontana, 1979) by Rose Elliot.

Jacaranda Wiley Ltd. for an extract from *The Macquarie Student Writer's Guide* (Jacaranda Press, 1989) edited by P. Peters.

Léon Jaeggi & Sons Ltd for an extract from *Le Répertoire de la Cuisine* (1914) by L. Saulnier.

Letts Educational for an extract from *Getting to Grips with Writing* (1992) by Catherine Hilton and Margaret Hyder.

Longman Group Limited for extracts from *Intermediate Language Skills: Writing* (1981) by M. Carrier, *Write for Business* (1987) by M. Doherty *et al.*, *Outlines* (1989) by A. Hopkins and C. Tribble, *Academic Writing Course* (1992) by R. R. Jordan, *Longman Dictionary of Applied Linguistics* (1985) by J. Richards *et al.*, *Process Writing* (1991) by R. White and V. Arndt, and *Writing for Business* (1983) by M. Wilson.

The McGraw-Hill Companies for an extract from *College Writing Skills with Readings* (1993) by J. Langan.

Macmillan General Books and the author c/o Rogers, Coleridge and White, 20 Powis Mews, London W11 1JN for an extract from *The Adventurous Fish Cook* (Macmillan, 1976) by George Lassalle, Copyright © Caroline Lassalle 1976, 1982.

Thomas Nelson Australia for model report and figures from *Writing Laboratory Reports* (1985) by Tony Dudley-Evans.

Oxford University Press for extracts and figures from *Writing, Intermediate* (1987) by M. C. Boutin *et al.*, *Writing* (1988) by T. Hedge, *Writing, Upper Intermediate* (1987) by R. Nolasco, *Headway Upper Intermediate* (1987) by J. Soars and L. Soars, *Writing, Advanced* (1987) by R. White, and one entry from *Oxford Advanced Learners Dictionary* (1989).

Oxford University Press, Inc. for extracts and figures from *Techniques in Teaching Writing* (1983) by Ann Raimes, Copyright © 1983 by Oxford University Press.

Phoenix ELT, a division of Prentice Hall International for extracts and figures from *Writing* (1994) by R. White and D. McGovern.

Prentice-Hall, Inc., Upper Saddle River, NJ, for a figure from *Writing Up Research* (1990) by R. Weissburg and S. Buker, © 1990.

J. Sainsbury plc and Martin Books, Simon & Schuster Consumer Group for an extract from *The Cooking of Tuscany* (1992) by Valentina Harris.

Taylor & Francis, Publishers, for the adapted list of prototypical genres from M. Callaghan, P. Knapp, and G. Noble: 'Genre in practice' in Bill Cope and Mary Kalantzis (eds.): *The Powers of Literacy: A Genre Approach to Teaching Writing* (Falmer Press, 1993).

Although every effort has been made to trace and contact copyright holders prior to publication some replies have not been obtained. If notified, the publishers will undertake to rectify any errors or omissions at the earliest opportunity.